immersed in the
s p l e n d o r

of GOD

resources for
worship renewal

F. Russell Mitman

THE
PILGRIM
PRESS
Cleveland

For my grandchildren, Montana Aubrey and Bo Morgan,
that they may discover being immersed in the splendor of God

Scripture quotations unless otherwise noted are from the New Revised Standard Version Bible, copyright © 1989 by the Division of Christian Education of the National Council of the Churches of Christ in the United States, and are used by permission.

The Pilgrim Press, 700 Prospect Avenue
Cleveland, Ohio 44115-1100, U.S.A.
thepilgrimpress.com

© 2005 by F. Russell Mitman

Printed in the United States of America on acid-free paper

10 09 08 07 06 05   5 4 3 2 1

Library of Congress Cataloging-in-Publication Data
Mitman, F. Russell.
    Immersed in the splendor of God : resources for worship renewal /
F. Russell Mitman.– [Rev. expanded ed.].
        p. cm.
    Rev. ed. of: Worship vessels. c1987.
    ISBN 0-8298-1614-3 (pbk. : alk. paper)
    1. Liturgies. 2. Liturgics. I. Mitman, F. Russell. Worship vessels. II. Title.
BV198.M57 2005
264 – dc22

                                                    2005042985

Contents

Preface

One ongoing responsibility of the parish minister is preparing weekly orders of worship. There are times in that process, as every pastor has discovered, when books of worship resources simply don't satisfy the needs of a particular service. There are also occasions when one of the great expressions of the tradition appears to need a language renovation or a new setting in order for it to remain authentic for worship today. Those are the moments that gave impulse to the worship resources in this book.

My former associate, the Reverend William R. Swisher, suggested a number of years ago that I put together an anthology of the resources I had prepared but, he insisted, not without some theological and liturgical introductions for the various acts of worship. His initial encouragement pushed me into a project that culminated in the publication of *Worship Vessels: Resources for Renewal* in 1987.

Nearly two decades have passed since the original materials were crafted, and the needs of churches have changed. It became clear that an update was in order, and I thank the editors of The Pilgrim Press for encouraging a thorough rewriting and the crafting of many new worship expressions for services of Word and Sacrament. Advances in desktop publishing now make possible what could not be done by the average worship leader two decades ago, and it became clear that any resources in book format also need to be available in electronic format as well. Hence, this volume includes most of the resources, including the music, on a CD-ROM from which they easily can be downloaded for insertion in bulletins and other media. It's hard to believe that the first manuscript was written the old-fashioned way — handwritten words in number 2 pencil on yellow legal pads that were then typed on a typewriter and copied! The world has changed, and this book has changed from its previous incarnation.

As the leader of a number of workshops in worship for pastors and laypersons, I discovered many years ago that one could not approach the task of liturgical renewal without first considering the structure of corporate worship. My subsequent stint as a teacher of worship in a theological school, decades consulting on worship with local church pastors and leaders, and ongoing visits to churches as part of my present position as Conference Minister only confirmed my findings. Hence the introductions to each of the chapters focus a great deal on the structuring and the interconnectedness of the various worship acts, traditionally referred to as the *ordo,* when Christians assemble to worship God.

The final chapter on bulletins is my attempt to treat a sadly neglected subject that is fundamental to all worship renewal in congregations of the free-church tradition. Corporate worship presupposes bulletins, even in an age of increased use of electronic media and tools, to enable the enactment of liturgy to take place.

In the process of creating worship resources during the past thirty or more years, I have borrowed from others as others have borrowed and will borrow from me. I have attempted to ensure that anything in this collection not of my own creation has been duly acknowledged. If something has slipped in otherwise, the inclusion is unintentional.

I wish to thank the congregation of the First United Church of Christ in Carlisle, Pennsylvania, for providing me with sabbatical leaves for the writing of the first edition of this book and for being receptive to testing some of these resources as part of their corporate worship experience. I also owe my gratitude to the pastors and local church leaders of Pennsylvania Southeast Conference of the United Church of Christ for allowing me the opportunities to facilitate workshops in a variety of settings, to consult with them regarding worship renewal in the churches, and to craft liturgies for monthly worship in the Church House and seasonal gatherings of the conference. Many of the new materials in this edition have arisen from the worship experiences in those settings.

I am deeply grateful to the copy editor, John Eagleson, for his care and sensitivity in the shaping of these liturgical materials in printed form and to Joseph Irwin Jr. for his assistance in preparing the accompanying CD-ROM.

Finally I thank my family for bearing with me so patiently without a renegotiation of my contract as husband and father during the first writing of this book when some were but children. And now as adults, they, together with my wife, Ruth, continue to encourage me to do the creative work that is so important to me and, hopefully, to the renewal of the worship life of the church.

Introduction

We have this treasure in earthen vessels.
— 2 Corinthians 4:7

Paul was writing to the Corinthians about ministry — his ministry and the whole church's ministry. He called this God-given empowerment a "treasure" (in Greek, *thesauros*) of spiritual gifts, gifts he enumerated at length elsewhere in the Epistles. "But," Paul said, "we have this treasure in *earthen vessels* [clay pots in NRSV] so that it may be made clear that this extraordinary power belongs to God and not to us" (emphasis added). The vessels and vehicles of ministry are very human ones, fashioned and shaped from the earth from which we have come and to which we shall return. God gives a rich treasure of grace, but we hold that treasury among us in forms and shapes that reflect the temporality and fragility of our humanness. Our earthenware existence reminds us that ministry is not of our own invention but is the gift of a transcendent God, who, in love, uses us as clay receptacles to receive and pass on the treasure. The first edition of this book in 1987 was titled *Worship Vessels: Resources for Renewal,* and my hope then, as now, was and is to offer some worship resources of my own shaping along with some needed introductions for their use.

A decade ago I was introduced to a remarkably gifted theologian and teacher, Marva J. Dawn. In the introduction to one of her volumes on worship she says that, in response to a certain theological and liturgical malaise in North American churches at the turn of the millennium, she envisioned a book that in its formative stages was titled *Immersed in Splendor.* In its final form the book was published as *A Royal "Waste" of Time: The Splendor of Worshiping God and Being Church for the World.*[1] In the introduction she writes:

> For a while this book was called *Immersed in Splendor.* I love the baptismal imagery in that phrase — like a plunge into a sapphire mountain lake on a hot day. Even so, worship is a cascade into the ever-flowing surprises of encounters wih the immensity of God's magnificence and sublimity and radiance. We have retained the word

1

splendor in the subtitle because worship that is a *royal* waste of time will immerse us in the fullness of God's sublime attributes and actions. That is why worship must be filled with all kinds of sounds, new music and old, faithful fountains of praise, powerful retellings of the biblical narratives, and ever-widening rivers to convey the grandeur of God.[2]

She concludes one chapter with this summary:

Style is not the issue. What matters is that whatever songs or forms we use keep us aware that God has invited us into worship, that God is present, that God is eminently worthy to receive our praise, and that there is so much to learn about that we will never get done. The question is whether our worship services immerse us in God's splendor.[3]

I am deeply indebted to Marva for allowing this wonderful image to shape the title of this edition. I hope that the vessels of worship that this book is about will be a faithful tribute to her work and will enable those who gather to worship, through these earthen vessels, to find themselves drawn into and immersed in the splendor of an awesome God.

What we have to do here, then, is a conversation about the forms and expressions we fashion and mold to receive and to pass on the extraordinary treasure of the good news. It will analyze how the people of God creates the forms and expressions for the ministry of corporate worship as well as provide some forms and expressions already shaped and ready for use. So it is both a set of introductions to the making of clay pots and a collection of pots I have made either by my own design or patterned after the examples of potters in the past. Everything here is either of my own crafting or is in the common domain. Therefore, through the marvels of electronic technology, these expressions can be downloaded directly from the accompanying CD-ROM. The purchase of this book and the accompanying CD-ROM grants permission for one-time use in a printed or electronic medium for corporate worship provided the acknowledgment on p. iv of this book is included. No additional permission or license needs to be secured.

There are available many collections of worship resources. Yet I always am curious: Why did certain potters fashion their earthen vessels in a particular way? What patterns were used in the creation of their forms and expressions? Since others may share the same curiosity, in the following chapters I will not only provide one more anthology of worship resources but also share the rationales that have been part of their creation.

Archeology has learned to use pottery as a means of fixing a certain culture in space and time. Another generation will produce earthen vessels patterned after those of their forebears, yet there will be a certain uniqueness of form and design not quite like that of previous eras. By providing a commentary on the forms and expressions in this book, I hope both to share with the reader the historic patterns that informed my making and to highlight any uniqueness fashioned here.

A piece of pottery is utilitarian and, as such, reflects the needs and signs of a given time. It is a utensil and not a timeless statue. In the same way, the forms and expressions in these chapters are meant to be used. They will be broken by use, and when no longer useful, they will be discarded. Although their design attempts to reflect a certain liturgical art endowed by Scripture and tradition, they are primarily intended to be forms and expressions that reflect the needs of the church in our time in the ordering of corporate worship. Their design has been informed by pastoral concerns that have arisen from the concrete situations of the life of worshiping congregations, and hence the needs that prompted their creation may not be universal. Thus, some of the forms and expressions will not be useful in some households of the faith, but we hope that others will be.

The resources in this book are not intended to replace others that have served well and, although antiques by time's standards, still remain viable for corporate worship today. I see these more as alternatives that can be used hand in hand with those of liturgical inheritance, especially in a day when a variety of lifestyles calls the church to provide for a variety of forms and expressions. Denominational liturgies need by nature to seek universality of expression and need to remain viable for at least a generation or two until new ones can be produced, authorized, and made indigenous to the church's life. The vessels herein, however, are alternate forms that may be appropriate only for occasional use and that can be disposed of even after being used just one time. Some may break apart very easily.

In fact, the history of liturgy points up how really fragile liturgical forms are and how free the church and individuals have been both to discard some vessels and to create more utilitarian ones. The Reformation of the sixteenth century created the need for a plethora of new liturgies. Calvin, for example, created many liturgies for different settings. He may have smashed into shards some of the revered liturgical antiques, yet at the same time he was free to preserve others and incorporate them quite successfully into new forms. The study of liturgy is a freeing experience that encourages individuals and churches to experiment liturgically. Our vessels are indeed very temporal expressions in an evolutionary process that has gone on before us and will continue long after both we and our vessels return to dust. And every so often in that process someone has the curiosity to search through the rubble and discovers a gem that begins to sparkle again in a new setting.

The designations of "contemporary" and "traditional," which we found exciting during the liturgical explosion of the sixties and have been revived in the "worship wars" of recent years, are for me both artificial and irrelevant. Worship is always a present and contemporary act — if our forms and expressions are authentic ones. Some so-called contemporary expressions are hardly worthy for the worship of God, and some traditional ones remain meaningful vessels of the treasure. The reverse is also true. Both new and old expressions may suffer from a poverty of language or an antiquarianism that makes them invalid. The reader will discover that some resources in this volume are lifted directly from the Bible and the liturgical history of the church. Most of these, however, are placed in a new or different setting — hence their inclusion here. Others are totally new. I hope both types of resources are valid, not because of their sources, but because the Christian community finds them to be authentic expressions of the divine-human interaction that the Bible witnesses to and the church has experienced since Pentecost.

Simultaneous to the publication of the first edition of this book, Neil Postman, educator and communications theorist, warned a culture addicted to the entertainment media that we are "amusing ourselves to death."[4] In the intervening two decades I have witnessed more and more the invasion of the entertainment mode into the worship life of churches. Choirs assemble themselves on the chancel steps to perform a musical piece, sometimes accompanied by electronically recorded orchestras too large to fit in person into the sanctuary itself. Children are rewarded for their performances with applause. Church chancels are renovated into stages or purpose-built as windowless sound sets devoid of symbols so that the visuals — and, hence the audience — can be controlled electronically. Huge television monitors display lyrics for congregational sing-alongs, sometimes visually accompanied by third-rate graphics and even cartoons, and the "message" is a computer-driven PowerPoint presentation. In much of what is marketed as "multimedia worship" the worshiper is engaged in a passive mode, that is, as an individual spectator watching and listening

to performers, either live or electronically recorded, without any significant involvement with anyone else. Or the focus becomes the personality
of the worship leader and his or her ability, in talk-show style and with
hand-held microphone pressed tightly to the lips, to engage the minds or
to excite the emotions of the audience. Sadly, all these measures are touted
by some consultants as essential to church growth, and too many threat-
ened clergy and lay leaders are being convinced that to counter decline
in attendance and membership they need to buy more technologically
sophisticated equipment and employ just a few more techniques of the
entertainment culture.

Yet there are some of us who believe with Marva Dawn that the focus
of worship is on God who is the Subject of worship.[5] From such a perspective worship, then, is a countercultural experience that, although it
may utilize some of the technology of the electronic age, nevertheless
has its primary focus on what *God* is doing and the responses that the
community assembled are making to the divine initiative. As in the biblical narratives, the discourse of such countercultural worship will be highly
metaphoric, allowing God to speak through the earthquake, wind, and fire
of the powerful biblical metaphors. There are some of us who are convinced through our interaction particularly with youth and young adults
that there are many people yearning for more than a flattened e-mail culture has given them, hoping for divine encounters that transport them
beyond the logics of physics, and looking for more breakthroughs of
meaning and purpose than a culture seduced by entertainment can deliver. They want to be met by a bush-burning God who will knock their
socks off and draw them into the mystery of the Holy One.

Since the very nature of this divine-human interaction is dialogical, the
forms we use to celebrate it are dialogues — call and response, question
and answer between God and us and also among members of the worshiping congregation. The Psalms are the classic examples of this form,
which is reinforced by the structure of Hebrew poetry wherein the statement of one line is restated in the second, parallel line. The Psalms were
intended to be sung responsorially. Hence the structure of many worship
expressions — both in history and especially today when printed bulletins
and electronic media become vehicles of common prayer — is essentially
a dialogue between leader and people. But there are other ways of ex-
pressing the dialogue, and the resources in this volume attempt to suggest
some different approaches.

Because liturgy is bound up with both the freedom and the constraints
of language, a word needs to be said regarding the language of worship.

The categories and themes that worship celebrates take their inspiration from the biblical story — creation, sin and forgiveness, redemption and reconciliation. Hence the language of worship will be different from the language of a political speech, a psychotherapy session, or a research paper. I often encounter worship materials that leave me with a less-than-satisfactory feeling simply because the language seems to be borrowed from another arena and cannot capture what worship intends to be about.

Moreover, since corporate worship, unlike private devotion, involves words spoken and meant to be heard and understood by others, liturgical expressions need to pass the test of being able to be spoken corporately. Words that appear quite beautiful and meaningful on paper sometimes cannot be spoken coherently by a group of people in worship. A certain inner rhythm and cadence is necessary to make corporate speaking possible and to keep it going. If we look to the models of the past, we find from the tradition of the Bible and the community of faith that the lasting expressions of worship exhibit a style informed by poetry and music. Again, the Psalms are the prime examples.

Any consideration of the language of worship also must wrestle with the problem of gender. In other Indo-European languages, especially the Greek and Latin that are the original languages of much of our liturgical inheritance, gender is a grammatical determination. This means that gender is determined by certain "classes" or "orders" of nouns and pronouns — and their corresponding adjectives. The word "gender" comes from the Latin *genus* meaning "order" or "classification." Originally, linguists tell me, all nouns were classified as either "common" or "neuter." The common classification, or *genus,* included all animate objects, and the neuter *genus* included all inanimate objects. What this means is that the language of worship comes to us from people who had a different linguistic perspective from what we who read and speak English have. This is true also of others who speak modern languages with a grammatical concept of gender. The ideas of "masculine," "feminine," and "neuter" are primarily *grammatical* rather than *sexual* classifications, as we sometimes assume in English.

All this leads to the point of clash: the question of inclusive language. Within recent years we have become aware of the need for sexual equality in the life of the church. In Christ there is no male or female. A problem arises when we seek to incorporate that need for justice in our liturgical expressions. The language we have inherited in worship, which is the language of the Bible and the early church, evolved in tongues with grammatical gender. When that language is adjusted to accommodate the church's agenda for sexual equality, we encounter difficulties with respect to language associated with the third person singular and plural — the singular primarily with respect to God, and the plural in reference to people.

In English we have no adequate generic word for the human situation. "Man" is weak, and, although grammatically generic — if there is such a thing in English — is too identical to the sexual "man" to be helpful. Both the Hebrew *adam* and the Greek *anthropos* are clearly generic, and some other modern foreign languages also have words generically differentiated from the sexual "man." The best we can do in English is to distinguish the generic liturgically by use of "people," which seems to preserve most often the biblical intention.

A larger crisis emerges when we deal with the language about God, and especially the pronouns for God. We have assumed that the "he" and "his" and "him" pronouns for God that we have inherited from earlier generations are sexually determined. With no concept of grammatical gender in English, that assumption is natural. In the classical languages in which our liturgical expressions were born, however, gender was grammatically determined, and hence the pronouns were grammatical ones. It is difficult to have a liturgy that is personal and relational without pronouns, especially in the style of Hebrew poetry such as we find in the Psalms. And there is the big question as to whether we can drop or find adequate substitutions for word concepts such as "Father," "Son," and "Lord," or to neuter "Christ" without deleterious theological consequences. The debate has continued for nearly two decades since the first edition of this volume. Some progress has been made, but there is still no ecumenical unanimity regarding language about God. And perhaps there never can be nor should be, for any words, any name, cannot contain the mystery of the One whose name is I-am-who-I-am.

Then there is the issue of updating the language of hymns and other liturgical expressions. Obviously editors of hymnals across the years have made editorial changes to suit the needs of the times. Translations from one language to another involve editorial decisions that can change radically the message. In this second edition I have made many language updates from those in the first edition. Generally I have attempted to change the "thee" and "thou" of hymn stanzas to "you" and "your." However, particularly in some memory-bank hymns, the need for rhyming would demand such significant changes that the theological meaning would be substantially changed. In those few instances I have preserved the traditional "thee" and "thou."

All this means that our liturgical expressions remain in a period of transition and development as we search for, test, and accommodate ways of using language to express what we believe. There is no easy solution. Liturgy needs both to reflect and to inform the life of faith. This process is always dialectic and always involves dialogue. I do not believe we can start from a predetermined agenda regarding theological and liturgical language. The language of worship is always being created, but that creation doesn't emerge from a vacuum. Authentic liturgy emerges from the process in which we attempt to express the divine-human interaction in words, and those words are never totally adequate to express the mystery of that interaction.

The goal of inclusiveness, at least in my mind, is to be truly catholic and to express and lift up universal worship for all people. If, however, we start from a set of experience-based criteria, the result may be sectarian — it may express the needs of one group but not of the whole church. Some recent liturgies suffer from a certain exclusiveness, ironically, in their very attempt to be inclusive. We need to be sensitive to the present needs for sexually inclusive language as we create new expressions, yet at the same time we need to honor those that come to us from a tradition that did not have the same cultural agendas (and language!) we have. My approach in this book is to provide both. Those who feel uncomfortable with certain usages may feel free to adapt them according to individual needs. And there are instances in which I provide for alternative wordings.

Most of the resources here are verbal ones — a restriction not intended to connote that liturgics is only a matter of words but necessitated by the medium of printing. Protestant worship, especially since the Enlightenment, has been overly verbal, and the process of renewal involves the discovery and rediscovery of many nonverbal forms and expressions. I have attempted, given the restrictions of a book, to indicate in the rationales and rubrics the possibilities for worship involving more of the senses and varied media of communication. However, it will be up to the reader and user of what is printed here to fill in the gaps. The resources here do not exclude the possibilities of other media, and, likewise, the use of these other media need not negate the verbal tradition either. Words in worship will be with us, I believe, for quite some time to come. Yet at the same time the needs of persons with visual and auditory handicaps need to be taken seriously so that corporate worship, which is primarily in words, will not exclude from the household of faith those who cannot see or read or hear words.

Some will see this collection primarily as a minister's handbook. If so, fine. But it is intended to be more than a book relegated to the minister's study. With the ease of duplicating processes — the whole of the final chapter is devoted to the possibilities at hand via bulletins — I hope that these resources will find their way into pews as well. The accompanying CD-ROM facilitates easy downloading of the expressions for insertion into whatever printed or electronic tool is used for corporate worship

Through the introductions at the beginning of each resource section I have attempted to provide an educational tool to arouse and to facilitate the study of worship and the preparing for worship in the local church. This intent is colored by my notion that liturgies are not only forms for worship but also vehicles for Christian education. I hope the commentaries will become a point of departure for clergy and laity to do some serious evaluation of present worship forms, to get some hold of the rationales that inform that process, and, finally, to create their own worship vessels. In order to provide some additional help to worship leaders in creating their own worship expressions, I have authored a companion volume, *Worship in the Shape of Scripture* (Cleveland: Pilgrim Press, 2001).

Notes

1. Marva J. Dawn, *A Royal "Waste" of Time: The Splendor of Worshiping God and Being Church for the World* (Grand Rapids, Mich.: Wm. B. Eerdmans Publishing Co., 1999).

2. Ibid., 7.

3. Ibid., 158.

4. Neil Postman, *Amusing Ourselves to Death: Public Discourse in the Age of Show Business* (New York: Penguin Books, 1986).

5. Marva J. Dawn, *Reaching Out without Dumbing Down* (Grand Rapids, Mich.: William B. Eerdmans, 1995), 76.

Chapter One

Word and Sacrament

The revolution in worship that took place during the 1960s left every congregation and worship leader wondering with greater or lesser degrees of anxiety about what happens in church during whatever hours are appointed on whatever days for the weekly worship of God. The forms once thought to be canonized by congregational tradition or correct liturgical scholarship all of a sudden a generation ago fell off the wall, and all the king's horses and all the king's men have not been able to put them back together again, at least not without the seams showing! Even the seemingly immutable Book of Common Prayer now has two sets of liturgies and collects from which to choose. It's interesting how, in most official denominational books of worship published recently or currently in the works, there is a subtle yet significant shift in terminology from "the" service to "a" service. Although worship has survived the explosion of the sixties, for the foreseeable future we have to accept the word "alternative" stamped on our worship forms. Sunday morning will never again see "the" appearing as a definite article to its forms. Maybe it never should have in the first place.

Before we go searching for viable and alternative expressions, however, we must begin with a fundamental question regarding the *structure* of the Lord's Day Service — that balanced pattern of Word and Sacrament, classically called the *ordo,* that is at the heart of liturgies, both ancient and modern, and is inherent in the divine-human interaction recorded in the Scriptures. I am continually amazed to see a parade of orders of worship that have about them a fresh sense of creative expression yet reflect an underlying structure quite inconsistent with those expressions. There are a number of books, of which this is one more, that have flooded pastors' studies with new resources for public worship. But most do not address the more important question, a question raised by a friend and pastor: How do I put the individual parts of the service together? A shopping list liturgy of creative expression is certainly no better — perhaps even much worse — than many of "the" liturgies that were abandoned some forty or

11

so years ago, and merely inserting new expressions into some of the old structures sometimes is tantamount to bolting a late-model fender onto an antique automobile. Both may have integrity in themselves, but they certainly don't structurally fit together. Therefore, we need first of all to address the question of the structure of the Sunday celebration.

There are a number of ways of getting at the structure, or *ordo,* of the Lord's Day celebration. I would like to reflect on three: the first two, although starting from different questions, arrive at a common structure; the third way may or may not be in harmony with the first two, depending on how it is utilized.

When we compare the Sunday services in a number of recent denominational liturgies, including the post–Vatican II mass, we discover to the astonishment of many that, except for variances in ceremony and uniqueness of linguistic expression, their structure is basically the same. All begin with some kind of introductory and penitential acts; all join together the reading and preaching of the Word as one act followed by intercessory prayers; all include an offertory; all continue with the celebration of the Holy Communion or Eucharist; and all conclude with a dismissal or sending into the world. That's putting one hour's worth into one sentence, but that's the basic structure of Sunday worship regardless of the label attached. Most Protestant services structure the service so that the Eucharist is normative for every Sunday but provide for an alternate ending if the Eucharist is not celebrated. There are not separate services for preaching and for Holy Communion.

What does this convergence mean? That we've all gone back to Rome? Yes, in that both Protestants and Roman Catholics have gone back to a common structure. No, insofar as this structure is akin to that of the *ordo* in the earliest church even before Rome became the head bishopric. The common structure of worship for the Lord's Day has a continuity throughout history. It's the same structure Wesley adapted from his revered Anglican Book of Common Prayer for use by American Methodists, the same structure of the Scottish, Dutch, German, and Swiss Reformed liturgies, the same structure of Luther's Deutsche Messe, the same structure of the mass in the days of Pope Gregory the Great, the same structure of the liturgies of the early Fathers, and the same structure that emerges in the New and Old Testaments themselves. Thus, not only do present-day liturgies find commonness among themselves but also the structure of any one of them is identical to that of any historical antecedent.

We can arrive at this commonness from another perspective, although from a different question and a different set of linguistic categories. Via this route the question becomes: When we are confronted by that which is beyond us, what happens? First, we experience an unsettling awareness of another presence, and we feel a need to acknowledge that we are not oblivious to that presence. This acknowledgment prompts a corresponding awareness of a fundamental difference between us and the other-than-us. Also, we yearn for some kind of reassurance that the difference is not irreconcilable, and hence, we sense a need for dialogue between us and the other-than-us. Once that need is met, we desire some kind of at-one-ness with this other-than us, and our desire isn't fulfilled until we are given some sign that the other-than-us has the same desire and that at-one-ness is complete. Finally, when we are satisfied that the confrontation is complete, we are able to say that it wasn't so bad after all!

The above interaction, although couched very much in human terms, describes, to me at least, what happens when God confronts us in worship. Although the language is different and the categories along this continuum are far more fluid than in a list of liturgical parts, it is my contention that the structure of such interaction is identical to that of the historic or contemporary liturgies outlined above and in the very shapes emerging from the biblical texts themselves. In another volume I provide a far more thorough discussion than can be elaborated here on the ways worship is shaped by Scripture.[1] Faithfulness to the divine-human interaction, as witnessed to in the Bible and in the liturgical history of the church, is the norm that results in a common order and the norm by which all liturgies, ancient and modern, are to be judged. Therefore, in response to my pastor friend's question regarding the putting together of the individual expressions, I can only say: Be faithful to the structure of the divine-human interaction. One can discover that structure by studying the liturgies that have survived the test of time, by taking a look at the commonness of many contemporary liturgies, and by analyzing carefully the structure of such biblical events as Abraham's call, Isaiah's temple vision, Mary's encounter with the angel Gabriel, or the Pentecost experience.

This brings us to the third way to structure worship for the Lord's Day. To Protestant minds the natural inclination is to look first to the Bible as the norm for worship, but I purposely have left this discussion until last because it needs to be approached carefully. There is an inherent difference between a biblical liturgy and a biblicistic one, and there is always the danger of attempting the first and ending up with the second. A biblical liturgy will reflect faithfully the intrinsic structure of the divine-human interaction, but it will not be satisfied with a collection of biblical passages strung together on the basis of a synthetic structure, foreign to the mode of the divine self-disclosure witnessed to in the Bible. It seems to me, for example, that a liturgy that places the offertory prior to the Scripture and sermon — as is still common practice in some corners of American Protestantism — does not reflect an understanding of the meaning of the offertory, nor of the reading of Scripture and the preaching of the sermon. Despite all the biblical language that can be compressed into one hour, such a structure is inconsistent with the Bible's record of the dynamics of what happens when God intervenes on the human scene. My notion is that such ordering is the result of ulterior motives. For example, I am acquainted with one church that placed the offering before the sermon so that the money could be counted during a much too lengthy sermon! In another church the sermon occurred after the celebration of the Eucharist so that the kids could go off to Sunday school while their parents attended to the more weighty stuff of the sermon. There was a lot of biblical language in both services, yet the liturgical structure seemed to obscure totally the mode of the divine-human interaction that is witnessed to so powerfully in the Bible.

A faithful structure of corporate worship will allow the dynamics of the divine-human relationship to be reflected in liturgical movement from beginning to end. All too frequently, however, the various parts of the service appear in the Sunday bulletin as a list of static categories. We will discuss the importance of the bulletin in the concluding chapter, but let it be sufficient to say here that the bulletin need contain only what is necessary to enable liturgical movement to take place. We don't need a detailed road map. Otherwise we'll spend most of our time with heads buried in the map and fail to see the scenery moving by us. Or, worse yet, in some services there's nothing going on anyway, so to alleviate the boredom we check the map periodically and dream of where we are supposed to go! When God confronts people, something happens: We are gathered, forgiven, talked to, listened to, nourished, commissioned, sent — all verbs. Likewise, when the weekly worship hour is over, we somehow ought to be aware that we are at a different place than we were an hour earlier. Physical movement heightens such awareness. I will attempt to demonstrate this in the resources that follow. For now, suffice it to say that faithful structuring of the service will reflect a sense of the spatial movement of the people of God in its pilgrimage on earth.

Faithful structuring also will reflect a sense of the movement of time. In a very real sense, the weekly worship hour is a microcosm of time, past and present and future. The biblical concept of time is linear; with a beginning, a midpoint, and an end. As the pilgrim people of God, we find ourselves at a particular time point in God's self-disclosure. Each worship time and each moment in that period of time is a new time that both remembers the past hours and moments and moves expectantly to the next moment and hour. A faithful structure will promote a kind of continual remembering of what has happened not only in the distant past but also last week, and earlier within the hour; and it will foster as well a continual questioning of what will happen in the next minutes and hours and days and weeks and years. The structure of the weekly worship time must be directed enough to bring about corporate and individual recollection, and open-ended enough to promote a sense of expectancy. Again, the bulletin cannot be a program in the literal sense of the word. It can only be a marker of what may happen in the future according to God's promise in the past. Our awareness of movement can be helped through adhering to the church year and the corresponding lectionaries. Although there is nothing sacred about the liturgical calendar and lectionary, they are disciplines to ensure we don't allow our own timepieces — and particularly the Reverend's — to become stalled on favorite moments and ideas. Those who find lectionaries too artificial may find the old Reformed idea of continuous reading of the books of the Bible verse by verse, chapter by chapter, in weekly installments more appropriate. Either method guarantees a certain movement and continuity in time from one week to the next.

Using a musical analogy, we may say that the movement and rhythm of Sunday's hour and of the liturgical seasons are like those of a symphony, which, paradoxically, needs no theatrics to be complete in itself. In other words, a structure that is faithful to the divine-human interaction will have an integrity of its own. Thus, although drama and music can reinforce liturgical rhythm and movement — and many examples that follow employ dramatic settings and musical elements — neither should be used to force coherence on the various liturgical expressions. One popular Sunday electronic church hour is quite sensuously appealing due to its flamboyant use of theatrical technology. The same can be said of some so-called "contemporary" services designed to attract generations addicted to the electronic media. However, when the theatrics are stripped away, the underlying structure is so disjunct and incoherent that it cannot possibly stand by itself. Without the lights and music and video screens the hour would be nothing more than a sermon with some randomly chosen opening and closing exercises. Liturgical integrity is tested by how we answer the question: Can this service stand without being propped up?

Professor Charles Rice says that there is still a lingering idea in American Protestantism that the sermon is "a kind of homiletical ocean liner preceded by a few liturgical tugboats."[2] Although this orientation is well fixed in the minds of some — particularly of preachers, it is really a novelty in the history of Christian worship. It received its canonization during the Enlightenment when ideas replaced actions. Thus, in an atmosphere where the primary question became, "What did the preacher say?" instead of, "What happened?" it was natural for the celebration of Holy Communion, like baptism, to be relegated to an ordinance. Scholarship in the latter decades of the previous century has enabled us to discover that the celebration of the Eucharist each Sunday is not a remnant of popery, but the norm of the churches who trace their heritage via Wesley, Knox, Calvin, Luther, Zwingli, and Cranmer. During the time of the Reformation, however, it was popular practice to commune infrequently (in most cases only once a year) even though the Eucharist was celebrated every Sunday as part of the mass. Therefore, it was difficult for the Reformers to get people to see the validity of communing each week. Also, because the focus of the Reformation was on the communal nature of the meal, none of the Reformers — given popular practice — could arouse sufficient support for the weekly celebration. The nineteenth century, under a new kind of historicism, saw a number of attempts at restoring the centrality of the Eucharist to each Sunday's celebration, but only a few were able to pull it off with any degree of success: namely, the Anglo-Catholic movement in the Protestant Episcopal Church and the newly formed Christian Church, commonly known as the Disciples of Christ, to mention the two most lasting.

In the last four hundred years we have barely inched our way from a semiannual or quarterly, to a sometimes monthly celebration of the Eucharist. Nevertheless, there are some significant breakthroughs in restoring the normative Sunday celebration of weekly Eucharist. The first is the liturgical practice that orders the service of the Lord's Day in such a way that the acts of the offertory symbolically point to the nourishing of God's people that occurs in the Eucharist. Whether or not the Eucharist is celebrated, the service each Sunday is the same up through the offertory. Following the offertory, when the Eucharist is not celebrated, the service concludes with the prayer of thanksgiving, the Lord's Prayer, and a dismissal. When the Eucharist is celebrated, the service begins the same but continues with the Eucharistic liturgy. This was the order of many of the Reformation liturgies, and it has been adopted by most recent denominational liturgies in a serious attempt to show the intrinsic unity of

Word and Sacrament and to say that this is the normative practice for every Sunday.

The second breakthrough comes from a pastoral perspective. Many of us have seen the increased desire of laypeople (clergy usually blame them for not wanting frequent Communion) to be fed and nourished by the Eucharist more than four times a year and more than once a month. I have discovered that there is a core of Christians who seriously want to receive the Communion weekly, and many of those are under thirty! Rather than forcing it upon those who are not ready to accept weekly Communion, we can provide for two alternative services each week: one in which the Eucharist is celebrated, and the other a service of the Word, so structured that when the Eucharist is included, the order up to the offertory is the same. These two approaches will enable the unity of Word and Sacrament to become more the norm than the exception and will allow those who desire weekly Communion to have their spiritual needs fulfilled.

Hesitantly, but for the sake of clarity, I include an outline of the structure of the service of Word and Sacrament (see the following page). The main headings correspond to the five chapters that follow, and the subheadings name the various acts for which resources are included. Still, a final note of caution is in order. As the reader will discover, sometimes in the following resources one act will flow directly into another. At other times, it may appear that a certain part is missing. At still other times one act may be substituted for another. I say all this to make it clear that the various parts of the service are not ends in themselves. They are parts of a larger whole — a living, dynamic event that happens when the people of God worship. Likewise, the structure is not an end in itself. It makes liturgy possible and enables the people of God to do the work of worship.

The resources in each of the following sections appear in the order of the church year — beginning with Advent and continuing to the end of the long season of Pentecost, or Kingdomtide. Within this general framework are resources for specific celebrations and expressions shaped by Scripture texts in the *Revised Common Lectionary*. In the introductory remarks to some of the resources, there are some suggestions for use on certain Sundays or festivals. However, I try to avoid the frequent assumption that a particular worship act is appropriate for only one Sunday or festival a year. If the worship leader begins by reading and studying the biblical texts that inform each Sunday's worship, the inspiration that prompted each of these worship vessels will emerge, I believe, and enable the leader to determine which resources best fit that worship service.

BASIC STRUCTURE OF A SERVICE
OF WORD AND SACRAMENT

———

GATHERING

Call to worship
Hymn or other act of praise

PENITENCE

Call to repentance
Prayer of confession
Words of assurance
Praise response

WORD

Prayer for illumination
Scripture lessons
Sermon
Affirmation of faith/Baptismal acts
Prayers of the people

OFFERTORY/EUCHARIST

When Eucharist is celebrated	*When Eucharist is not celebrated*
Offertory, including presentation of elements	Offertory
Eucharistic prayer	Prayer of thanksgiving
Breaking the bread and pouring the cup	
The Lord's Prayer	The Lord's Prayer
Distribution	
Post-communion thanksgiving	

SENDING

Charge and/or Blessing
Closing Hymn
Departure

A final word needs to be said about the music that is either suggested or included in the resources. Most hymn texts were written apart from the music to which either the authors or composers themselves have wedded their texts or to which hymnal editors over time have set the texts. Obviously there has been considerable editing of texts, and over time some tunes have become more popular than others with respect to certain hymn texts. In Great Britain, for example, "O Little Town of Bethlehem" is generally set to the English folk tune FOREST GREEN, while in the United States most people sing it to ST. LOUIS. In some instances I have suggested alternate tunes for some hymn texts. Generally hymn tunes have names that are printed in small capital letters. These are listed at the back of most hymnals in the "Tune Index." In some instances I have indicated in the resources themselves the tune to which I suggest the hymn texts be sung. However, the worship leader may think otherwise and is free to change tunes to suit congregational familiarities. Because of copyright issues, some texts and music I suggest cannot be reproduced without separate permission. Hence I simply make some suggestions of possibilities. However, all music that I have composed or which is in the public domain may be downloaded from the CD-ROM and printed in worship bulletins with the accompanying permission indicated above.

Notes

1. F. Russell Mitman, *Worship in the Shape of Scripture* (Cleveland: Pilgrim Press, 2001).

2. Charles Rice, *The Embodied Word: Preaching as Art and Liturgy* (Minneapolis: Fortress Press, 1991), 31.

Chapter Two

Gathering

There are a myriad of ways by which the people of God are gathered and come together on the Lord's Day. We are not a mighty army all marching in step to the same cadence, but a pilgrim band straggling and struggling through the valleys and over the mountains following the call of God. Our gathering sometimes may be prompted by an inner hunch that amid this pilgrimage is the promise of *Shalom*. Sometimes, too, it's a recollection of past promises that draws us as individuals to find a common bond with our brothers and sisters in the covenant of grace. Sometimes our mood is festive, and with joy we hurry our steps to be numbered with those who are invited to the banquet. Sometimes we find ourselves together for some inexplicable reason. Sometimes changes in life situations nudge individual seekers inside worship spaces and within worshiping communities for the first time in their lives, and they find themselves entering into a strange new world where the sounds and sights are almost terrifyingly foreign. Lots of times most folks are in the pews because they've always been there. I affirm the validity of all these reasons for gathering and maintain that our gathering acts ought to reflect a diversity of expressions suitable to the setting and meaning of each particular celebration and provide a worship hospitality that welcomes even the first-time visitor. However, *all* gathering acts, whether enacted at the font or leading to the font, reflect that the Christian life and worship in the assembly of gathered Christians begins in baptism and in remembrance of baptism. The commonly used Trinitarian baptismal formula ("In the Name of the...") and dipping hands into water and making the sign of the cross on the forehead are verbal and tactile reminders that all worship begins in the bath of immersion into the splendor of God.

Many of the gathering acts in this anthology are verbal, and some are accompanied by congregational singing. Yet it needs to be said that nonverbal approaches, although more subliminal, are equally valid. The sounding of the *shofar* is an ancient but powerful call for the people of God to gather. Likewise, in Pacific-rim cultures blowing the conch shell signals that worship is beginning. Bells in many religious traditions call people to worship; in others drums. Nonvocal music, silent processions where only the footsteps convey the message, projected pictures and images, interpretive movement, and other symbolic acts all have historical precedents and contemporary validity as acts of gathering. Depending on the circumstances, a number of nonverbal acts may be combined with verbal ones for a powerful statement that the people of God are coming together by the prompting and invitation of a gracious and welcoming God.

A processional (and corresponding recessional) is, in essence, a non-verbal statement that we are a pilgrim people on the move, coming from somewhere and going on to another place and time. As I have attempted to preserve in some of the following, processionals were integral settings for many of the Psalms. Palm Sunday's story in the New Testament is the account of a processional, and unless we physically move on Palm/Passion Sunday, we may miss the meaning of the biblical message.

However, there are a couple of processional pitfalls into which we have fallen as we have sought to bring respectability to worship and have viewed it as an aesthetic experience. Processionals and recessionals are not machinery for getting choirs in and out of lofts. The danger is always to use the procession every Sunday and thereby to destroy its inherent integrity. Far worse is marching the choir and clergy in time to the hymns. Such rigidity practically eliminates the singing of all hymns other than those in 2/4 or 4/4 time and nonverbally says that we are a pompous people parading to the beat of our own drums. To those who have processed into a rut, I urge a moratorium on processionals; to those who have never attempted one, I suggest an occasional processional when appropriate to the meaning of the day. In addition, I want to say that processionals need not be restricted to choir and clergy. There are occasions such as dedications and festivals when all or part of the congregation can be on the move accompanied by visual symbols such as banners, lights, processional crosses, musical instruments, and obligato voices. It is important, however, to ensure that ceremony does not mask the real meaning of our gathering. A slavish concern for things ceremonial can reduce liturgy to a collection of obscure rubrics that after a while require commentaries to be understood.

At the other end of the spectrum is the simple call to worship God or the informal greeting of one another or the responsive versicle of Scripture. All are appropriate gathering acts that acknowledge that God is present and that the divine-human interaction has begun. The setting, the occasion, and the number of persons present will dictate what act is most appropriate.

CALLS TO WORSHIP _____

The following act is designed to be a processional for the Advent season. The physical movement of the procession symbolizes the movement of the people of God to a new day. A reader or the minister may read the Scripture passages from Micah 4:1–3 while processing with the choir. Except for the last stanza, the hymn should be sung unaccompanied by solo voice and choir. It is best also for the "Rejoice" responses to be sung in unison.

◆◆◆   2.1.1

Solo: O come, O come, Emmanuel, and ransom captive Israel,
          That mourns in lonely exile here, until the Son of God appear.

Choir: Rejoice! Rejoice! Emmanuel shall come to you, O Israel!

Solo: O come, O Dayspring, come and cheer our spirits by your Advent here;
          Disperse the gloomy clouds of night, and death's dark shadows put to
              flight.

Choir: Rejoice! Rejoice! Emmanuel shall come to you, O Israel!

The choir begins processing.

Leader: In the days to come the mountain of the Lord's house shall be established
          as the highest of the mountains, and shall be raised up above the hills;
          Peoples shall stream to it, and many nations shall come and say:

All: **"Come, let us go up to the mountain of the Lord,**
          to the house of the God of Jacob;
          that he may teach us his ways and that we may walk in his paths."

The congregation may stand.

Leader: For out of Zion shall go forth the law,
          and the word of the Lord from Jerusalem.

Solo: O come, O Wisdom from on high, and order all things far and nigh;
          To us the path of knowledge show, and help us in that way to go.

Choir: Rejoice! Rejoice! Emmanuel shall come to you, O Israel!

Leader: He shall judge between many peoples,
          and shall arbitrate between strong nations far away;
          they shall beat their swords into plowshares,
          and their spears into pruning hooks;
          nation shall not lift up sword against nation,
          neither shall they learn war any more.

All: *With accompaniment, last phrase as an introduction*
O come, Desire of Nations, bind all peoples in one heart and mind.
Bid envy, strife, and quarrels cease; fill all the world with heaven's
    peace.
Rejoice! Rejoice! Emmanuel shall come to you, O Israel!

Leader: Come, let us walk in the light of the Lord!   —Isaiah 2:5

◆◆◆   2.1.2

*The following includes both gathering and penitential acts. The hymn stanzas suggested
here are those of the seventeenth-century German pastor Johannes Olearius as translated
by Catherine Winkworth. The tune, PSALM 42, is from the Genevan Psalter of 1551. Two
alternatives are offered for the words of assurance: either the spoken words of Isaiah 40:1, 9, or
a soloist singing the paraphrase of the same text. In either case the congregation joins to sing
the final hymn stanza. A more contemporary set of stanzas from the hymn "There's a Voice
in the Wilderness" by J. Lewis Milligan as set to the tune ASCENSION may be substituted
for the more traditional stanzas printed here.*

Leader 1: A voice cries out:

Leader 2: In the wilderness prepare the way of the Lord,
make straight in the desert a highway for our God.
Every valley shall be lifted up, and every mountain and hill be made low;
the uneven ground shall become level, and the rough places a plain.
Then the glory of the Lord shall be revealed,
and all people shall see it together,
for the mouth of the Lord has spoken.   —Isaiah 40:1–5

The congregation may stand.

All: *Singing*   PSALM 42
Now the herald's voice is calling in the desert far and near,
bidding us to make repentance since the reign of God is here.
O that clarion call obey! Now prepare for God a way;
Let the valleys rise in meeting and the hills bow down in greeting.

Leader 1: A voice says, "Cry out!"

Leader 2: And I said, "What shall I cry?"

Leaders 1 & 2:
All people are grass, their constancy is like the flower of the field.
—Isaiah 40:6

All: In the wilderness where we find ourselves, O God,
    constancy is hard to come by.

We feel tossed to and fro by culture's every whim and wind;
  in the midst of the world's many words,
  it is difficult to discern the One Word that seeks to be heard.
In the lonesome desert we feel isolated,
  cut off from the sacred springs;
  we are like the grasses of the fields —
  flowering today, gone tomorrow.
Confession is so difficult to speak, for we know not what to confess;
  forgiveness so hard to receive, for we ourselves cannot forgive.
Lord, have mercy on us!
Christ, have mercy on us!
Lord, have mercy on us!

Silence

Alternative 1:

Leader 1: Comfort, O comfort my people, says your God.
  Speak tenderly to Jerusalem, and cry to her
  that she has served her term,
  that her penalty is paid,
  that she has received from the Lord's hand double for all her sins.

Leader 2: Get you up to a high mountain, O Zion, herald of good tidings,
  lift it up, do not fear;
  say to the cities of Judah, "Here is your God!"   —Isaiah 40:1, 9

Alternative 2:

Soloist: "Comfort, comfort O my people, tell of peace," thus says our God;
  Comfort those who sit in darkness bowed beneath oppression's load.
  Speak unto Jerusalem of the peace that waits for them;
  Tell them that their sins I cover, and their warfare now is over.

All: *Singing*   PSALM 42
  Straight shall be what long was crooked, and the rougher places plain!
  Let your hearts be true and humble, for Messiah's holy reign.
  For the glory of the Lord now o'er earth is shed abroad;
  And all flesh shall see the token that God's word is never broken.

◆◆◆ 2.1.3

In the following call to worship the leader may speak in a loud voice, almost shouting, at the rear of the sanctuary or in a balcony.

Leader: In the wilderness prepare the way of the Lord,
  make straight in the desert a highway for our God.

All: Every valley shall be lifted up,
    and every mountain and hill be made low;

Leader: The uneven ground shall become level,
    and the rough places a plain.

All: Then the glory of the Lord shall be revealed,
    and all people shall see it together,
    for the mouth of the Lord has spoken. —Isaiah 40:3–5

◆◆◆ 2.1.4

Leader: Say to those who are of a fearful heart,
    "Be strong, do not fear. Here is your God who comes to save you."

All: Then the eyes of the blind shall be opened,
    and the ears of the deaf unstopped;
    Then the lame shall leap like a deer,
    and the tongue of the dumb sing for joy. —Isaiah 35:4–6

An appropriate hymn to follow is Charles Wesley's "O For a Thousand Tongues to Sing,"
especially the stanza so often missing from many hymnals:

  Hear him, you deaf, you voiceless ones, your tongues again employ;
  You blind, behold your Savior comes; and leap, you lame, for joy!

The last stanza:

  Glory to God and praise and love be ever, ever given
  by saints below and saints above, the church in earth and heaven

may be reserved to be sung following the confession and words of assurance as a praise response.
This stanza also may be used generally as a doxology.

◆◆◆ 2.1.5

The following includes a unified gathering and penitential act. Although the tune for
"O Little Town of Bethlehem" suggested here is KINGSFOLD, *the words may also be sung*
to the more traditional tunes, ST. LOUIS *or* FOREST GREEN. *The periods of silence should be*
generous. If a choir is present to assist congregational singing, the final stanza may be sung
a cappella.

Leader: But you, O Bethlehem of Ephrathah, who are one of the little clans of
    Judah, from you shall come forth for me one who is to rule in Israel,
    whose origin is from of old, from ancient days. Therefore Israel will
    be abandoned until the time when she who is in labor gives birth; then
    the rest of his kindred shall return to the people of Israel. And he shall
    stand and feed his flock in the strength of the Lord, in the majesty of

the name of the Lord his God. And they shall live secure, for now he shall be great to the ends of the earth; and he shall be the one of peace.

—Micah 5:2–5a, NRSV and NIV

All: *Singing*   KINGSFOLD
O little town of Bethlehem, how still we see you lie!
Above your deep and dreamless sleep the silent stars go by;
Yet in your dark streets shines forth the everlasting light,
The hopes and fears of all the years are met in you tonight.

For Christ is born of Mary, and gathered all above,
while mortals sleep, the angels keep their watch of wondering love.
O morning stars, together proclaim the holy birth!
And praises sing, and voices ring with peace to all on earth.

Words: Phillips Brooks, 1868, alt.

All: *Speaking*
Your Bethlehem this Advent is surrounded, O God,
 by less than a holy silence,
  and a world at war still waits for the promised peace to come.
The hopes and dreams of all the years
 are shattered by remembrances of violence,
  and the thought of yet more terror barricades us in our fears.
We can barely look out to the horizon,
 barely reach out without trembling.
The dread of scarcity scares us into stinginess,
 and bells calling us to generosity
 are deafened by the tinnitus
 of our world's moral and spiritual malaise.
Dear God, we are crazed by the roaring madness,
 there is no health in us,
 and we yearn for just a respite of sacred silence.

Silence

Leader: *Speaking or singing in a whisper*
How silently, how silently, the wondrous gift is given!
So God imparts to human hearts the blessings of his heaven.
No ear may hear his coming, but in this world of sin
where yearning souls receive him, still the dear Christ enters in.

Silence

All: *Singing*
O holy Child of Bethlehem, descend to us, we pray.
Cast out our sin, and enter in, be born in us today.
We hear the Christmas angels the great glad tidings tell;
O come to us, abide with us, Our Lord Emmanuel!

◆◆◆ 2.1.6

The following is to be sung antiphonally by the congregation and a solo voice. It is best for the soloist to be at some distance. Those desiring to use a more inclusive form may substitute "watcher" for "watchman."

Tune: ABERYSTWYTH or ST. GEORGE'S WINDSOR

All: **Watchman, tell us of the night, what its signs of promise are.**

Soloist: Traveler, O a wondrous sight! See that glory-beaming star!

All: **Watchman, does its beauteous ray news of joy or hope foretell?**

Soloist: Traveler, yes, it brings the day, promised day of Israel!

All: **Watchman, tell us of the night, higher yet that star ascends.**

Soloist: Traveler, blessedness and light, peace and truth its course portends.

All: **Watchman, will its beams alone gild the spot that gave them birth?**

Soloist: Traveler, ages are its own; see it bursts o'er all the earth!

All: **Watchman, tell us of the night, for the morning seems to dawn.**

Soloist: Traveler, darkness takes its flight, doubt and terror are withdrawn.

All: **Watchman, let your wand'rings cease; hasten to your quiet home.**

Soloist: Traveler, now the Prince of peace, now the Son of God has come.

Words: John Bowring, 1825, alt.

◆◆◆ 2.1.7

If the following is used as a processional, a banner may precede the procession. If a crèche is placed in the sanctuary, a child may place the figure of the Christ child in the manger during the reading, "For to us a child is born...." There is no need for an introduction to stanzas 2 and 3. A simple pedal note on the organ will suffice. A vocal or instrumental descant may accompany the last verse. It is best to omit a final "Amen."

Choir: *A cappella*
O come, let us adore him,
O come, let us adore him,
O come, let us adore him, Christ, the Lord!

The congregation may stand.

All: *Singing with accompaniment*
O come, all ye faithful, joyful and triumphant,
O come ye, O come ye to Bethlehem;
Come and behold him, born the King of angels;

O come, let us adore him,
O come, let us adore him,
O come, let us adore him, Christ, the Lord!

Leader: The people who walked in darkness have seen a great light;
          those who dwelt in the land of deep darkness, on them has light shined.

All: **For to us a child is born, to us a son is given;**
          and the government will be upon his shoulder,
          and his name will be called "Wonderful Counselor,
          Mighty God, Everlasting Father, Prince of Peace!"   —Isaiah 9:6

All: *Singing*
          Sing, choirs of angels, sing in exultation,
          Sing, all ye citizens of heaven above!
          Glory to God, all glory in the highest;
          O come....

Leader: And the Word became flesh and lived among us;

All: **We have seen his glory, glory as of a father's only son,**
          **   full of grace and truth.**   —John 1:14

All: *Singing*
          Yea, Lord, we greet thee, born this happy morning,
          Jesus, to thee be all glory given;
          Word of the Father, now in the flesh appearing.
          O come....

◆◆◆   2.1.8

This Epiphany call to worship may be followed immediately with the singing of the hymn "Arise, Your Light Is Come" by Ruth Duck. Another possibility is William Dix's "As With Gladness Men of Old," or the more inclusive version, "As With Gladness Those of Old."

Leader: Arise, shine; for your light has come,
          and the glory of the Lord has risen upon you.

All: **For behold, darkness shall cover the earth,**
          and thick darkness the peoples;

Leader: But the Lord will arise upon you,
          and his glory will appear over you.

All: **And nations shall come to your light,**
          and kings to the brightness of your dawn.   —Isaiah 60:1–3

◆◆◆ 2.1.9

In the following the period of silence is an enactment of the Scripture text and should be generous enough for personal prayer. When it is time to continue speaking the Psalm, the leader simply begins reading, "God alone . . ." and the congregation will follow automatically. No verbal rubrics are necessary. An accompanying penitential act may be found at 3.2.34.

Leader: The Lord is in the holy temple;
         let all the earth keep silence before God!   —Habbakuk 2:20, adapt.

**All: For God alone my soul waits in silence,
         for my hope is from God.**

Silence

**God alone is my rock and my salvation, my fortress;
I shall not be shaken.
On God rests my deliverance and my honor;
my mighty rock, my refuge is in God.**

Leader: Trust in God at all times, O people;
         pour out your heart before God who is our refuge. —Psalm 62:5–8, adapt.

The Psalm paraphrase "God is Our Refuge and our Strength" is an appropriate hymn to continue the gathering.

◆◆◆ 2.1.10

Leader: This is the day the Lord has made!

All: Let us rejoice and be glad in it!   —Psalm 118:24

Leader: This is the hour when the true worshipers
         will worship the Father in spirit and truth.

**All: God is spirit, and those who worship him
         must worship in spirit and truth.**   —John 4:23–24, adapt.

Leader: This is the moment when we encounter the living God
         and experience God's presence among us.

All: Let us worship God!

◆◆◆ 2.1.11

Minister: The grace of our Lord Jesus Christ,
           the love of God,
           and the communion of the Holy Spirit
           be with all of you.   —2 Corinthians 13:13

All: And also with you.

Minister: Let us give one another a sign of our life together in Christ.

All may greet one another and/or exchange the Peace of Christ.

Minister: Let us worship God.

◆◆◆   2.1.12

The following gathering act is based upon Psalms 100 and 122, both of which inspired the hymn stanzas by William Kethe, Isaac Watts, and Thomas Ken. The tune to which all three writers set their verses is the familiar OLD HUNDREDTH *from the Genevan Psalter. If the act is used as a processional, it is likely that the choir will enter the chancel area during the reading, "And now our feet are standing within your gates." The initial stanzas may be sung unaccompanied by the choir. The dynamics and sense of movement are heightened even more if the final doxology is sung with a vocal or instrumental descant. An alternative adaptation in inclusive language was prepared by Thomas Troeger and may be substituted for these traditional words.*

Choir: All people that on earth do dwell
sing to the Lord with cheerful voice;
Him serve with mirth, his praise forth tell;
come ye before him and rejoice!

Leader: Know that the Lord is God.
It is God who made us, and not we ourselves.

People: **We are the Lord's, the people of God, the sheep of God's pasture.**
—Psalm 100:3, adapt.

Choir: O enter then his gates with praise,
approach with joy his courts unto;
Praise, laud, and bless his name always,
for it is seemly so to do.

Leader: I was glad when I heard them say: "Let us go to the house of the Lord."

All: **And now our feet are standing within your gates, O God!**
—Psalm 122:1–2, adapt.

Following the organ interlude the congregation stands and joins in singing:

All: **We'll crowd thy gates with thankful songs,
High as the heavens our voices raise;
And earth with her ten thousand tongues,
Shall fill thy courts with sounding praise!**

**Praise God, from whom all blessings flow!
Praise him, all creatures here below!
Praise him above, ye heavenly hosts!
Praise Father, Son, and Holy Ghost! Amen.**

◆◆◆   2.1.13

Psalm 91 is appointed several times in the Revised Common Lectionary, *one of which is for the First Sunday in Lent. Here it is juxtaposed with Luther's hymn "A Mighty Fortress is Our God." An inclusive language adaptation has been prepared by Ruth Duck. It is interesting for the Leader 2 sentences to be spoken by a female voice.*

Leader 1:   You who live in the shelter of the Most High,
who abide in the shadow of the Almighty,
will say to the Lord,

All: **My refuge and my fortress;
my God in whom I trust.**   —Psalm 91:1–2, adapt.

The hymn is sung.

Leader 1:   Because you have made the Lord your refuge,
the Most High your dwelling place,
no evil shall befall you, no scourge come near you.
For God will command angels concerning you
to guard you in all your ways.
On their hands they will bear you up,
so that you will not dash your foot against a stone.

Leader 2:   Those who love me, I will deliver;
I will protect those who know my name.
When they call to me, I will answer them.
                                   —Psalm 91:9–12, 14–15, adapt.

◆◆◆   2.1.14

Leader: God proves love for us in that while we still were sinners
Christ died for us.   —Romans 5:8

All: **Behold the lamb of God who takes away the sin of the world!**
                                   —John 1:29, RSV

◆◆◆   2.1.15

The following includes both gathering and penitential acts. It is appropriate throughout the Lenten season and Holy Week. A crucifix or cross may be carried in processional during the singing of the first hymn stanza. Yes, the opening Scripture call to worship is repeated again as the assurance of forgiveness.

Leader: The message about the cross is foolishness to those who are perishing,

All: **but to us who are being saved it is the power of God.**
                                   —1 Corinthians 1:18

Leader: Let us worship God.

All: *Singing*   ST. CHRISTOPHER
        Before your cross, O Jesus, our lives are judged today;
        the meaning of our eager strife is tested by your way.
        Across our restless living the light streams from your cross,
        and by its clear, revealing beams we measure gain and loss.

All: *Speaking*
        Before your cross, O Jesus,
        we find ourselves judged, tested, measured.
        What we have done and have left undone stand judged before a cross
        that renders a final verdict on the ways of sin and death.
        The strife between sisters and brothers, between nations and cultures,
        that wounds your sacred body
        and tears apart our human community
        is tested before a cross that signs a way so counter to our ways.
        Our appetite for bigger and better, for stronger and more powerful,
        is measured by a cross that counts all as loss
        for the sake of faithfulness to the reign and power of God.
        Before your cross, O Jesus,
        we find ourselves judged, tested, measured.

Silence

All: *Singing*   ST. CHRISTOPHER
        The hopes that lead us onward, the fears that hold us back,
        our will to dare great things for God, the courage that we lack,
        The faith we keep in goodness, our love, as low or pure,
        on all, the judgment of the cross falls steady, clear, and sure.

The congregation may stand.

        Yet, humbly, in our striving, we rise to face its test.
        We crave the power to do your will as once you did it best.
        On us let now the healing of your great Spirit fall,
        and make us brave and full of joy to answer to your call.

                              Hymn stanzas: Ferdinand Q. Blanchard, 1929

Leader: The message about the cross is foolishness to those who are perishing,
        but to us who are being saved it is the power of God. —1 Corinthians 1:18

All: **Thanks be to God who gives us the victory through our Lord Jesus Christ.**

◆◆◆   2.1.16

Leader: Blessed is the One who comes in the name of the Lord!

All: **Hosanna in the highest heaven!**   —Matthew 21:9

◆◆◆ 2.1.17

One well-loved hymn that comes from the German pietist tradition is Paul Gerhardt's "O How Shall I Receive You." In many hymnals it is set to the tune ST. THEODULPH, *a very march-like melody familiar to another Palm Sunday hymn, "All Glory, Laud, and Honor." Generally "O How I Shall I Receive You" is located in the Advent section of most hymnals, but one can see readily that it is quite suitable for Palm Sunday as well, especially when sung to* ST. THEODULPH.

The hymn appears below in a Processional for both Advent and Palm Sunday. The prophetic call of Isaiah, announced by three readers, is juxtaposed with Gerhardt's very personal words, which are sung by the entire congregation. Since the message of Palm Sunday is essentially that of a procession, it is quite appropriate for the celebration of Palm Sunday to begin in a processional. However, the same thing can be said about Advent.

All that needs to be printed for congregational response are the words of the hymn with some indication that reading will take place between the verses. With the choir leading the singing, it is not necessary to give introductions to each verse; a single organ pedal note will suffice. It is interesting to add a trumpet descant at the last verse.

The reading may begin at the sanctuary door.

Reader 1: Get you up to a high mountain,
             O Zion, herald of good tidings!

Reader 2: Lift up your voice with strength, O Jerusalem,
             herald of good tidings! Lift it up, fear not!

Reader 3: Say to the cities of Judah, "Behold your God!"

The congregation may stand, and the choir begins processing.

All: *Singing*
             O how shall I receive you, how meet you on your way,
             The hope of every nation, my soul's delight and stay?
             O Jesus, Jesus, give me now by your own pure light,
             To know whate'er is pleasing and welcome in your sight.

Choose one of the two sections for Advent or Palm Sunday:

Advent:

Reader 1: Behold, the Lord God comes with might,
             and his arm rules for him;
             Behold, his reward is with him,
             and his recompense before him.   —Isaiah 40:10, RSV

Reader 2: He will feed his flock like a shepherd,
he will gather the lambs in his arms;
he will carry them in his bosom,
and gently lead those that are with young.   —Isaiah 40:11, RSV

Palm Sunday:

Choir: Blessed is the One who comes in the name of the Lord!
Hosanna, hosanna in the highest!   —Matthew 21:9

Children may process with palm branches and place them on the altar table or in another appropriate location as the congregation sings:

All: *Singing*
**Your children palms are strewing and branches fresh and fair.
My soul, in praise awaking, its anthem shall prepare.
Perpetual thanks and praises forth from my heart shall spring;
And to your name the service of all my powers I bring.**

On both occasions the act continues:

All: *Singing*
**Love caused your incarnation, love brought you down to me;
Your thirst for my salvation procured my liberty.
O love beyond all telling, that led you to embrace,
In love all love excelling, our lost and fallen race!**

Reader 3: How beautiful upon the mountains
are the feet of the messenger who announces peace,
who brings good news, who announces salvation,
saying, "Your God reigns!"   —Isaiah 52:7

All: *Singing*
**Christ who alone can cheer you is standing at the door,
He brings his pity near you, and bids you weep no more.
He comes, who contrite sinners will with the children place,
The children of his Father, the heirs of life and grace.**

◆◆◆   2.1.18

By the latter part of the fourth century, Christians in Jerusalem began Holy Week by gathering on the Mount of Olives in the afternoon. The Gospel narrative of Jesus' triumphal entry was read, and a procession into the city was enacted with children carrying palm or olive branches. In the Revised Common Lectionary *the Gospel lessons for Palm/Passion Sunday accounts are joined with the continuation of the whole passion narrative. The following liturgy for gathering is simply a reenactment of the Palm Sunday narrative according to Matthew. A liturgical reenactment of the continuing passion narrative, including the Lord's Supper, may be found at number 6.1.7.*

Leader 1: When they had come near Jerusalem and had reached Bethphage, at the Mount of Olives, Jesus sent two disciples, saying to them,

Leader 2: "Go into the village ahead of you, and immediately you will find a donkey tied, and a colt with her; untie them and bring them to me. If anyone says anything to you, just say this, 'The Lord needs them.' And he will send them immediately.'"

Leader 1: This took place to fulfill what had been spoken through the prophet, saying,

Leader 3: "Tell the daughter of Zion, Look, your king is coming to you, humble, and mounted on a donkey, and on a colt, the foal of a donkey."

Leader 1: The disciples went and did as Jesus had directed them; they brought the donkey and the colt, and put their cloaks on them, and he sat on them. A very large crowd spread their cloaks on the road, and others cut branches from the trees and spread them on the road. The crowds that went ahead of him and that followed were shouting,

All: *Shouting*
Hosanna to the Son of David!
Blessed is the one who comes in the name of the Lord!
Hosanna in the highest heaven!

The singing of the hymn "Ride On! Ride On in Majesty" by Henry Milman may continue the story. Children may carry palm branches and scatter them in the aisles.

Leader 1: When he entered Jerusalem, the whole city was in turmoil, asking, "Who is this?" The crowds were saying,

All: **"This is the prophet Jesus from Nazareth in Galilee."**

—Matthew 21:1–11

This may be followed immediately by a simple penitential act consisting of periods of silence each followed with the words, "Jesus, remember me when you come into your kingdom" (Luke 23:42) or as set to music by Jacques Berthier.

◆◆◆ 2.1.19

Leader: The Lord is risen!

All: **He is risen indeed!**

Leader: The kingdom of the world has become the kingdom of our Lord and of his Christ,

All: **And he will reign forever and ever!**   —Revelation 11:15

◆◆◆ 2.1.20

In the following, asperges, that is, the act of sprinkling water from a bowl of water with a pine or spruce bough, may accompany the opening words. The words, "Remember your baptism, and give thanks!" may be repeated each time the water is sprinkled. Likewise the corporate amen may be repeated following the sentence. An accompanying penitential act may be found at number 3.2.19.

Leader(s): Our worship is in the Name of the Triune God.
Remember your baptism, and give thanks!

All: **Amen!**

Leader: All of us who have been baptized into Christ Jesus
were baptized into his death,
so that, just as Christ was raised from the dead,
we too might walk in newness of life. —Romans 6:3–4, adapt.

The hymn "We Know That Christ Is Raised and Dies No More" by John Brownlow Geyer is appropriate here not only in Eastertide, but throughout the church year.

◆◆◆ 2.1.21

The following includes both the gathering and penitential acts as a unified whole. It is designed for use on the Fourth Sunday of Easter, commonly known as "Good Shepherd Sunday." Here the tune suggested for the hymn is LAUDA ANIMA, *although the more traditional* BRADBURY *also may be used. If* BRADBURY *is used, the final line must be repeated.*

Leader: Jesus said:
I am the good shepherd. I know my own and my own know me....
And I lay down my life for the sheep. —John 10:14–15

All: *Singing* LAUDA ANIMA
Savior, like a shepherd lead us, much we need your tender care;
In your pleasant pastures feed us, for our use your folds prepare.
Blessed Jesus, blessed Jesus, you have bought us, yours we are;

We are yours, in love befriend us, be the guardian of our way;
keep your flock, from sin defend us, seek us when we go astray.
Blessed Jesus, blessed Jesus, hear your children when we pray.

Leader: Let us pray.

All: **Shepherding Savior, much we need your tender care.**
We have strayed from your ways like lost sheep.
We have left undone those things we ought to have done,
And we have done those things we ought not to have done.
We are lost in the wildernesses of our own making,

And the wholeness we so passionately seek continues to elude us.
Blessed Jesus, find us, and carry us home.

Silence

Leader: Listen to the comforting assurance of the grace of God:
"Christ himself bore our sins in his body on the cross, so that, free from
sins, we might live for righteousness; by his wounds you have been healed.
For you were going astray like sheep, but now you have returned to the
shepherd and guardian of your souls." —1 Peter 2:24–25

All: **Thanks be to you, Lord Jesus Christ!**

All: *Singing:* LAUDA ANIMA
Let us always seek your favor; let us always do your will;
Jesus Christ, our only Savior, with your love our spirits fill.
Blessed Jesus, blessed Jesus, you have loved us, love us still.
Words: Dorothy A. Thrupp (1779–1847), alt.

◆◆◆ 2.1.22

Leader: O come, let us sing to the Lord;

All: **Let us make a joyful noise to the rock of our salvation!**

Leader: Let us come into God's presence with thanksgiving;

All: **Let us make a joyful noise to God with songs of praise!**

Sing a joyous hymn of praise.

Leader: O come, let us worship and bow down,

All: **Let us kneel before the Lord, our Maker.**

Leader: For the Lord is our God,

All: **And we are the people of God's pasture,**
and the sheep of God's hand. —Psalm 95:1–3, 6–7, alt.

Follow immediately with a unison prayer of confession.

◆◆◆ 2.1.23

*Here a portion of Psalm 100 is juxtaposed with Benjamin Schmolck's hymn as translated
by Catherine Winkworth. Stanzas of a new translation by Madeleine Forell Marshall, "Let
Me Enter God's Own Dwelling," may be substituted for those printed here. The lines of
the psalm may be spoken individually by three persons, or they may be said together by one
person. The leader(s) should speak powerfully and joyfully. The tune is* UNSER HERRSCHER.

If used as a processional, the initial call and stanza 1 may be sung from the rear, with the choir beginning to process as the leader(s) speaks: "Go within his gates...." A soprano or instrumental descant will heighten the intensity in stanza 3, and a rousing Amen will provide a joyous conclusion.

Leader 1: Cry out with joy to the Lord, all the earth!

Leader 2: Serve the Lord with gladness!

Leader 3: Come before God singing for joy!

The congregation may stand.

All: *Singing*
         Open now the gates of beauty, Zion, let me enter there,
         Where my soul in joyful duty waits for God who answers prayer:
         O how blessed is this place, filled with solace, light, and grace!

Leader 1: Enter God's gates with thanksgiving!

Leader 2: Enter God's courts with songs of praise!

Leader 3: Give thanks and bless God's name!

All: *Singing*
         Gracious God, I come before Thee, come Thou also down to me;
         Where we find Thee and adore Thee, there a heaven on earth must be:
         To my heart, O enter Thou, let it be Thy temple now.

Leader 1: The Lord is good;

Leader 2: God's steadfast love endures for ever,

Leader 3: God's faithfulness to all generations!

All: *Singing*
         Speak, O Lord, and I will hear Thee, let Thy will be done indeed;
         May I undisturbed draw near Thee, while Thou dost Thy people feed.
         Here of life the fountain flows, here is the balm for all our woes.
         Amen.

◆◆◆ 2.1.24

The following call to worship is designed for Pentecost. Since the event as recorded in Acts 2 involved speaking in known languages, the sentence, "I speak about God's deeds of power," should be spoken amid the congregation, one after another, by persons who can read the passage in different languages. Each person may want to add a one-sentence personal testimony to the Spirit's power. The person speaking in English should begin.

Leader 1: "In the last days it will be, God declares,
           that I will pour out my Spirit upon all flesh,

and your sons and your daughters shall prophesy,
and your young men shall see visions,
and your old men shall dream dreams." —Acts 2:18

Leader 2: When the day of Pentecost had come, they were all together in one place.
And suddenly from heaven there came a sound
like the rush of a violent wind,
and it filled the entire house where they were sitting.
Divided tongues, as of fire, appeared among them,
and a tongue rested on each of them.
All of them were filled with the Holy Spirit,
and began to speak in other languages, as the Spirit gave them ability.
—Acts 2:1–2, 4

Each speaks in a different language:

I speak about God's deeds of power.... —Acts 2:11b, adapt.

As soon as the last person has spoken, the congregation sings a joyous Pentecost hymn-prayer imploring the Holy Spirit to come. Suggestions are: the final stanza, "O Spirit, sent from heaven...," of Jane Parker Huber's "On Pentecost They Gathered"; or, "Wind Who Makes All Winds That Blow" by Thomas Troeger; or, "Like the Murmur of the Dove's Song" by Carl P. Daw Jr.

◆◆◆　2.1.25

Leader: Come to Christ, that living stone, rejected by mortals
but in God's sight chosen and precious;
and like living stones let yourselves be built into a spiritual house;
for you are a chosen generation, a royal priesthood, a holy nation,
God's own people, that you may declare the wonderful deeds
of the one who called you out of darkness into God's marvelous light!

All: **Once we were no people, but now we are God's people!**
—1 Peter 2:4, 5, 9, RSV, adapt.

Continue by singing "Christ Is Made the Sure Foundation."

◆◆◆　2.1.26

Leader: Our worship is in the name of the Father,

All: **The one eternal God in whom we live and move and have our being,**

Leader: And of the Son,

All: **Our crucified and risen Lord, Jesus Christ,
through whom the love of God is made manifest among us,**

Leader: And of the Holy Spirit,

All: **The Counselor by whom we are renewed the people of God
and the Church of Jesus Christ.**

◆◆◆   2.1.27

*The following includes both the gathering and penitential acts. The prayer is shaped by
the story of Elijah's encounter with God in 1 Kings 19, which is coupled in the* Revised
Common Lectionary *with Psalm 42.*

Leader: Our worship is in the Name of the Father,
and of the Son, and of the Holy Spirit.

or

Leader: Our worship is in the Name of the Triune God.

and   Remember your baptism and give thanks!

All: **Amen.**

*The leader may pour a bowl of water and invite those who desire to dip their fingers into the
water and to make the sign of the cross on their foreheads or on the foreheads of others. A
musical setting of Psalm 42 such as "As Pants the Hart for Cooling Streams" or "As Deer
Long for the Streams" may be sung either by a choir, a soloist, or the assembly.*

Leader: As a deer longs for flowing streams,

All: **so my soul longs for you, O God.**   —Psalm 42:1

Leader: Our souls yearn for you, O God, for the living God.

All: **We have wandered through wildernesses,
seemingly chased by powers beyond our control.
We do not know what we are doing here in this holy place,
yet we come with a remembrance of water once poured on us,
and the sign of grace that through baptism
we belong to Christ and to one another.
So we come emotionally tired and spiritually exhausted,
to find the living water
that once again will drench the dryness of our souls.
Immerse us in your splendor, O God,
and give us what we need for the rest of our journey.**

Silence

◆◆◆ 2.1.28

Leader: At the name of Jesus every knee shall bow,
in heaven and on earth and under the earth,

All: **And every tongue shall confess that Jesus Christ is the Lord,
to the glory of God the Father.** —Philippians 2:10–11, adapt.

◆◆◆ 2.1.29

Many of the Psalms were sung antiphonally in ancient Israel. Psalm 136, even in translation, preserves the antiphonal structure. John Milton's paraphrase of Psalm 136, "Let Us with a Gladsome Mind," is an excellent hymn to be sung in this manner. Except for the last stanza, the congregation needs to learn only one line, which can be printed in the bulletin along with the music for that line. It is set here along with the call and assuring words from Isaiah 42. The hymn is generally set to either MONKLAND *or* INNOCENTS. *Either setting is appropriate for antiphonal singing; however, both the solo and congregational melody lines are the same in* INNOCENTS. *A brief interlude will afford the opportunity for the congregation to stand and be prepared to sing the final stanza. Thomas Troeger has crafted an alternative set of words, "Let Us with a Joyful Mind," which may be substituted.*

Solo: Let us with a gladsome mind praise the Lord who is so kind.

All: **For God's mercies shall endure, ever faithful, ever sure.**

Leader 1: Thus says God the Lord,
who created the heavens and stretched them out,
who spread out the earth and what comes from it,
who gives breath to the people upon it,
and spirit to those who walk in it:

Leader 2: "I am the Lord. I have called you in righteousness.
I have taken you by the hand and kept you;
I have given you as a covenant to the people,
a light to the nations, to open eyes that are blind,
to bring out the prisoners from the dungeon,
from the prison those who sit in darkness." —Isaiah 42:5–7

Solo: God with all-commanding might filled the new-made world with light.

All: **For God's mercies shall endure, ever faithful, ever sure.**

Leader 2: "I am the Lord, that is my name;
my glory I give to no other, nor my praise to idols.
See, the former things have come to pass,
and new things I now declare;
before they spring forth, I tell you of them." —Isaiah 42:8–9

Solo: All things living God does feed; with full measure meets their need:

All: For God's mercies shall endure, ever faithful, ever sure.
Minister: Sing to the Lord a new song,
Sing God's praise from the end of the earth! —Isaiah 42:10

During the interlude the congregation may stand.

All: Let us with a gladsome mind, praise the Lord who is so kind.
For God's mercies shall endure, ever faithful, ever sure.

◆◆◆ 2.1.30

Leader: Jesus said: "I am the bread of life.
Whoever comes to me will never be hungry,
and whoever believes in me will never be thirsty." —John 6:35, adapt.

The congregation may stand.

All: *Singing* CWM RHONDDA
Guide me, O my great Redeemer, pilgrim through this barren land;
I am weak, but you are mighty; hold me with your powerful hand.
Bread of heaven, Bread of heaven,
feed me till I want no more, feed me till I want no more.

Open now the crystal fountain, where the healing waters flow.
Let the fire and cloudy pillar lead me all my journey through.
Strong deliverer, strong deliverer,
ever be my strength and shield, ever be my strength and shield.
Words: William Williams, 1745, alt.

Leader: In the wilderness, God commanded the skies above,
and opened the doors of heaven.
God rained down manna to eat and gave the grain of heaven.

All: For no one lives by bread alone,
but by every word that proceeds from the mouth of God.
—adapted from Psalm 78:23–24, Deut. 8:3

Leader: Let us pray.

All: O Provider of today's bread
and Promiser of tomorrow's essentials:
We come to you confessing a preoccupation with getting and keeping
rather than giving and sharing.
A richness in things masks our poorness in soul,
and an abundance of possessions
distracts us from a poverty in spirit.
We invest our fortunes in earthly stores,
but fail to claim an interest in heaven's treasures.

Yet, O God, you call us to an accounting of our of lives
and to an audit of our values.
In our bankrupted spirituality
we stand in the court of your judgment and grace,
admitting how dependent we are on you,
begging you to forgive our sinful self-sufficiency,
and asking you to fill our hungering emptiness
with a life of more than bread alone. Amen.

Leader: Jesus said, "Do not work for the food that perishes,
but for the food that endures for eternal life.
The bread of God is that which comes down from heaven
and gives life to the world."

All: Lord, give us this bread always.   —John 6:27, 33–34, adapt.

◆◆◆ 2.1.31

*In the following a portion of Psalm 96 is juxtaposed with a stanza of a metrical paraphrase
of the same Psalm by Charles H. Gabriel. The tune suggested here is* OLD HUNDREDTH,
although the words may be sung to most any other long meter tune, one of which is GONFALON
ROYAL *by Percy Buck. If the latter is used, a wonderful concluding Alleluia will be included.*

Leader: O sing to the Lord a new song;
sing to the Lord, all the earth!

All: **Sing to the Lord, bless God's name;
proclaim God's salvation from day to day.**

Leader: Declare the Lord's glory among the nations,
The Lord's marvelous works among all the peoples!

All: **For great is the Lord and greatly to be praised,
to be feared above all gods.**

Leader: For all the gods of the peoples are idols;
but the Lord made the heavens.

All: **Honor and majesty are before the Lord
in whose sanctuary are strength and beauty.**

Leader: Worship the Lord in holy splendor;
tremble before the Lord, all the earth!   —Psalm 96:1–6, 9

All: *Singing*   OLD HUNDREDTH
**Let every tongue and every tribe
give to the Lord due praise and sing;
All glory unto God ascribe,
Come, through the courts, and praises bring.**

◆◆◆   2.1.32

Psalm 150 has inspired the writing of many vocal and instrumental compositions. The following setting calls for the inclusion of instrumental sounds, yet it does not require lengthy preparations and rehearsals. A very brief fanfare or flourish by each instrument is all that is necessary; and only one cymbal crash, please! Each should last no more than three or four seconds, and there should be no breaks between readings and instrumental sounds. Players should be ready; quick timing is essential. It is best for instrumentalists to be situated throughout the congregation, and each reader should be located next to his or her corresponding instrumentalist. All should stand after the assembly says, "Praise God for surpassing greatness!"

Leader: Praise the Lord! Praise God in the sanctuary!

All: Praise God in the mighty firmament!

Leader: Praise God for mighty deeds!

All: Praise God for surpassing greatness!

Reader 1: Praise God with trumpet sound! (*trumpet*)

Reader 2: Praise God with lute and harp! (*guitar, harp, or autoharp*)

Reader 3: Praise God with tambourine and dance! (*tambourine*)

Reader 4: Praise God with strings and pipe! (*flute or recorder*)

Reader 5: Praise God with sounding cymbals! (*finger cymbals*)

Reader 6: Praise God with loud crashing cymbals! (*cymbals*)

Leader: Let everything that breathes praise the Lord!

All: Praise the Lord!

Sing "Praise the Lord, God's Glories Show" or other hymn of praise.

◆◆◆   2.1.33

The following call to worship is inspired by the ancient sursum corda, *"Lift up your hearts," of the Eucharistic liturgy. For a further short treatise see number 6.1.16.*

Leader: Lift up your hearts!

All: We lift them up to the Lord.

Leader: Lift up your eyes!

All: We lift them up and look to the Lord, our God.

Leader: Lift up your hands!

All: We lift them up and call on the name of the Lord.

Leader: Lift up your voices!

All: We lift them up and sing for joy!

The sursum corda *also inspired the hymn "Lift Up Your Hearts" by Henry M. Butler. Set to the tune* WOODLANDS, *it is a wonderful way to continue this gathering act.*

◆◆◆ 2.1.34

In the following the hymn stanzas serve as a prayer of invocation.

Leader: How lovely is your dwelling place, O Lord of hosts!

All: My soul longs, indeed it faints for the courts of the Lord;
             my heart and my flesh sing for joy to the living God.   —Psalm 84:1–2

All: *Singing*   TALLIS CANON
             Unto your dwelling place we come to praise you, God, most holy,
             and pray that this may be our home until we touch eternity.

             Come dwell with us now in this place,
                 you and your Christ to guide and bless.
             Here make the wellsprings of your grace
                 like fountains in the wilderness.

             May your whole truth be spoken here, your Gospel light forever shine.
             In sacraments to us draw near, and share with us your gifts divine.
                                              Words: Robert Collyer, 1873, alt.

◆◆◆ 2.1.35

The following is designed for harvest or thanksgiving celebrations. The invocation is based upon Psalm 67. The musical portions also may be spoken responsively by a reader and the congregation. The unison portion is adapted from the Book of Common Prayer.

Leader: Worship the Lord in the beauty of holiness!

All: Let the whole earth stand in awe of God!

The congregation may stand.

Leader: O God, be gracious and bless us,
             and let your face shed its light upon us.
             that your way may be known upon earth,
             your saving power among all nations

Cantor:

Let   the   peo - ples   praise   you,   O   God.

Choir and/or Congregation:

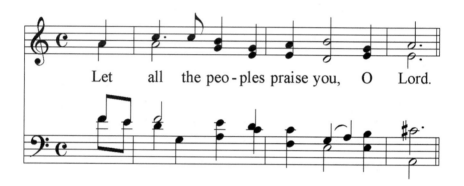

Let   all   the peo - ples praise you,   O   Lord.

Leader: Let the nations be glad and sing for joy,
          for you rule the world with justice,
          and guide the nations on earth.

Cantor: Let the peoples praise you, O God,

Choir and/or congregation:
          Let all the peoples praise you, O Lord.

Leader: The earth has yielded its fruit,
          God, our God, has blessed us.
          May God continue to bless us;
          let all the ends of the earth revere God.

Cantor: Let the peoples praise you, O God,

Choir and/or congregation:
          Let all the peoples praise you, O Lord.

**All: Almighty God, unto whom all hearts are open,
          all desires known, and from whom no secrets are hid:
          cleanse the thoughts of our hearts
          by the inspiration of your Holy Spirit,**

that we may perfectly love you
and worthily magnify your holy name;
through Christ our Lord. Amen.

◆◆◆ 2.1.36

Leader: God is our refuge and strength, a very present help in trouble.

All: The Lord of hosts is with us; the God of Jacob is our refuge!

Leader: Come, behold the works of the Lord!
See what amazing things God has done on earth!

All: The Lord of hosts is with us; the God of Jacob is our refuge!
—Psalm 46:1, 7, 8, 11, adapt.

This may be followed with a singing of "A Mighty Fortress Is Our God."

◆◆◆ 2.1.37

All: Sing to the Lord, all the earth.

Leader: Sing to the Lord and bless God's holy name;

All: Proclaim the good news of God's salvation from day to day.

Leader: Honor and majesty are before the Lord;

All: Strength and beauty are in God's sanctuary.

Leader: Worship the Lord in the beauty of holiness;

All: Let the whole earth tremble before God.

Leader: Tell it out among the nations: "The Lord is King!"
—Psalm 96:1–3, 6, 10, adapt.

This may be followed with the singing of "Praise, My Soul, the King of Heaven," "Worship the Lord in the Beauty of Holiness," or "Rejoice, the Lord Is King."

◆◆◆ 2.1.38

The following setting of a portion of Psalm 47 begins with the Leader establishing a steady clapping cadence. The Psalm verses also may be said in unison. Note that the last three lines beginning with "Sing," "For," and "Sing," begin <u>before</u> the clap, and the two concluding claps are syncopated. This may take some practice, particularly with the choir!

		(clap)		(clap)		(clap)		(clap)	
Leader:		Clap	your	hands,	all	peo-		ple!	x

		(clap)		(clap)		(clap)		(clap)	(clap)
		Shout	to	God	with	shouts	of	joy,	x

		(clap)		(clap)		(clap)	(clap)
Choir or All:	Sing	praises	to	God,	sing	praises	x

		(clap)		(clap)		(clap)		(clap)	(clap)
Leader:	For	God	is	King	of	all	the	earth;	x

		(clap)		(clap)		(clap)	(clap) (clap)
Choir or All:	Sing	praises	to	God with a	psalm!		x x

—Psalm 47:1, 6–7, adapt.

This may be followed with the singing of "Sing Praise to God Who Reigns Above" or the folk hymn "All You Peoples, Clap Your Hands."

Chapter Three

Penitence

Ever since the Enlightenment the idea of confession of sin has had an aura of suspicion, neglect, and sometimes ambivalence, especially on the American church scene. To free churches, confession of sin has smacked of dogmatism and popery, and thus it has been abandoned; to rationalists and pentecostals, it is unnecessary and therefore forgotten; to revivalists, it became part of the conversion machinery, and by having sins spelled out sins can be avoided. To most church people, confession of sin conjures up strange feelings.

A reading of the confessions of sin in the liturgies of the sixteenth-century Reformation leaves the impression that the sometimes lengthy recital of sins was the result of a gloomy preoccupation with this three-letter word. However, to Luther, Calvin, Knox, and their contemporaries, sin was present in the day-to-day struggle against sin institutionalized, the power of which could and did lead Christians to their deaths. Things were rotten and needed to be confessed to the Almighty. In an age of later rationalism — and I will not date it — this very real awareness is often construed and interpreted as being merely the gloomy metaphysics of Teutonic minds.

Yet it was the reality of a Great War and its slaughter that aroused Barth and others on the Continent and the Niebuhrs and others on the American scene to the very real power of sin. Following the second war with the same combatants, confessions of sin appeared again in the Sunday bulletins of churches; and during the 1960s, many church people could identify sins public and private just as well as their Teuton ancestors. After Vatican II, the Roman Catholic Church brought confession out of the closet and made it public in the mass itself. Interestingly, at about the same time, Karl Menninger and others in the psychology camp also began to wonder whatever happened to the three-letter word.

Whether we come to approach the concept of sin from the perspective of theology, psychology, history, or politics, we can agree that there is an unsettledness about human life, a feeling both corporate and private

that something is awry. Evil is still very real even though it is couched in
ideas, forms, and institutions that are essentially benign in intent Hence
our awareness, despite prophetic voices, is not immediate, and thus, in
disguise, sin may be even more powerful. In its more overt form, particularly since the events of September 11, 2001, evil has become personified
and linked to terrorists and terrorist organizations. Thus, our own com-
plicity with evil forces can be ignored, and the need for justice often is
transformed unapologetically into a thirst for vengeance. Guilt, too, is still
very real to most people, although often it is hidden by our inability to face
up to it. Moreover, in an age when violence is rationalized and justified, it
is hard for people to recognize their own need to receive forgiveness from
others and from God. I get the feeling that despite the horrible recital of
how wretched they were, the Reformers of the sixteenth century had a
far greater awareness than we do of a self-worth that is assured by a God
who graciously forgives.

In worship, it seems appropriate that following our acknowledgment
that the divine-human interaction has begun, there needs to be some kind
of penitential act in which our unsettledness with the human condition
cries out for *Shalom*. "Sin," as the English translation of the New Testament Greek *hamartia,* has its origin in military language: it is what
happens when the archer draws the bow, lets the arrow fly, but misses the
mark. This missing-of-the-mark that God intends for us is fundamentally
far more than some mere errors of judgment or even wilful misdoings. To
sin is to be and therefore to do what *God* does not intend for God's creatures to be and to do. Sin is a breaking of the essential Creator-creature
relationship: we are human and not God, and in the presence of the Divine, we find ourselves, like the first creatures, standing nakedly human
before the God who finds us in our hiding. Such fundamental estrange-
ment cries out for acknowledgment, appeals for forgiveness, and needs to
receive the promise of restoration. Therefore, a penitential act is corporate
and individual; it is invocation and confession together; it is asking for the
healing God has promised and for the healing we need from each other;
it is the assurance that restoration of the divine-human relationship shall
be; and it is giving thanks and praise both for the promise of *Shalom* and
for the *Shalom* given to us in the act itself. That is the reason I prefer to
speak of one penitential act, which, depending on the circumstances, may
include any or all of the traditional divisions of invocation, call to confession, confession of sin, the ancient *Kyrie* ("Lord, have mercy"), assurance
of pardon, and the words of a praise response such as a psalm, canticle,
hymn, or the traditional *Gloria in Excelsis*. Hence, in some of the worship

forms here and in the accompanying CD-ROM, various expressions are joined to create a unified whole.

The penitential act also involves more than words. It is a time for all the emotions. It is singing and speaking and silence. It is sitting, kneeling, standing, and other body movements. It may even be the time for congregational greeting as a sign of corporate *Shalom,* even though the giving of peace is traditionally part of the Eucharist.

Some question whether confession should be postponed until after the Word, since it is the Word that moves us to penitence and confession. That, indeed, may be appropriate on occasions, but it also can be asked: Why not an introductory penitential act and another as part of the Eucharist? For example, the Eucharist service in the Book of Common Prayer and Wesley's redaction include the general confession as part of the Eucharist and have an introductory penitential act in the form of the collect for purity. I have structured liturgies in which it seemed appropriate to have the penitential act as part of the offertory and Eucharist. I have structured others, especially services of ante-communion, in which the penitential act appears in its more traditional setting. In still others, there is both an introductory act of penitence and a confession as part of the Eucharist. In a service that includes the act of laying on of hands for healing, the penitential act may seem most appropriately placed following the Word act as a preface to the healing liturgy. Again, the nature of the celebration should guide the placement.

Integral to the penitential act, wherever it takes place, is the twofold action of confessing sin and asking for forgiveness. The second half is as important as the first. The *Kyrie* comes from the earliest Greek Church and is frequently appended to or becomes part of the prayer for confession. Whether said or sung, it is a humble way of asking God for mercy.

The penitential act concludes with some sign of acknowledgment and appropriation of forgiveness. This usually takes the form of verses of Scripture with or without the announcement that upon the promise of God we are forgiven. It is *God* who absolves, and the leader's role is simply to announce the promise as witnessed to in the Scriptures. The action is completed with words of praise and thanksgiving, which may include psalms spoken or sung, canticles, the traditional *Gloria in Excelsis,* or a simple "Thanks be to God!"

CALLS TO REPENTANCE _____

◆◆◆ 3.1.1

Leader: When we come into the holy presence of God,
our own humanity is laid bare.
When we stand in the living presence of truth,
our own falsehood is revealed.
People of God, let us acknowledge who we are
and ask our ever-present God to forgive us.

◆◆◆ 3.1.2

Leader: To prepare ourselves for Christ to come,
let us return to God with sincere and penitent hearts,

All: **For God is gracious and merciful,
and is always ready to forgive**.   —based on Joel 2:12–13

◆◆◆ 3.1.3

Leader: Before the mystery of the Word made flesh,
let us approach with faith,
bow down in reverence,
and offer our humble confession.

◆◆◆ 3.1.4

Leader: Humble yourselves under the mighty hand of God,
so that God may exalt you.
Cast all your anxiety on God
Because God cares about you.   —1 Peter 5:6–7, adapt.

◆◆◆ 3.1.5

Minister: If then we have been raised with Christ,
let us set our hearts on the things of heaven where Christ is
and put behind us the earthly things in which we once walked.
Let us confess our sin.   —paraphrased from Colossians 3:1ff.

◆◆◆ 3.1.6

Leader: Since we have a great High Priest, Jesus the Son of God,
who in every respect has been tested as we are,

All: **Let us therefore approach the throne of grace with boldness
that we may receive mercy and find grace
to help in time of need.** —Hebrews 4:14–16, adapt.

◆◆◆ 3.1.7

Leader: Dear friends in Christ, we gather this hour to worship God
and to be nourished by Word and Sacrament.
In the presence of each other and with the Holy Spirit to help us,
let us make our humble confession to God and to one another,
that we may be forgiven and be made whole again.

◆◆◆ 3.1.8

Leader: If we say we have no sin, we deceive ourselves,
and the truth is not in us.

All: **But if we confess our sins, God who is faithful and just,
will forgive our sins and cleanse us from all unrighteousness.**
—1 John 1:8–9

◆◆◆ 3.1.9

Leader: Beloved brothers and sisters,
let us draw near to God in all sincerity and confess our sins,
asking God in the name of Jesus Christ to grant us forgiveness.

PRAYERS OF CONFESSION _____

◆◆◆ 3.2.1

This prayer may be spoken in its entirety, or the hymn stanza may be sung in unison, a cappella.

**Lord, come to us as a way through the wilderness of life.
Come to us, for the mountains we need to climb seem much too high
and the valleys through which we must pass seem much too deep.
Come to us, for life is rough and rugged.
Come to us, Lord, with a new way.
Come to us with a child to show us the way.**

**O come, O come, Emmanuel, and ransom captive Israel!
That mourns in lowly exile here, until the Son of God appear.
Rejoice! Rejoice! Emmanuel shall come to you, O Israel!**

◆◆◆   3.2.2

O God, you have made us children of light;
   but we have chosen the road of shadows and darkness.
You have prepared the way for yourself and for others,
   but we have been content with ourselves
   and indifferent to the needs of others.
O God, bring forth a new shoot of life from the stumps of our dried-up souls
   and our desert-like world.
Reveal your glory to us
   that we may have the courage to look up and to hope again. Amen.

◆◆◆   3.2.3

The Kyrie *portion of the following may be said or sung responsively, or a single "Lord, have mercy upon us" may be substituted for the* Kyrie, *and the entire prayer may be prayed in unison.*

Leader: O God, whose will to be with us
         causes us to fall humbly on our knees;

All: **Forgive our wanting instead of waiting,**
         our taking instead of receiving
         our using instead of preparing.

Leader: Lord, have mercy upon us.

All: **Lord, have mercy upon us.**

Leader: Christ, have mercy upon us.

All: **Christ, have mercy upon us.**

Leader: Lord, have mercy upon us.

All: **Lord, have mercy upon us.**

Leader: O come, O come Emmanuel!

All: **And by your coming free our imprisoned hearts**
         and our chained-up minds,
         that a new promise may stir our tired world
         to rejoice again in the hope of a new day dawning;
         through Jesus Christ our Lord. Amen.

◆◆◆   3.2.4

The following may be preceded with the singing of "O How Should I Receive You?" The final "Amen" may be sung.

Leader: O holy and hidden God, you come knocking for us to receive you,

All: **yet we close tight the doors of our minds and hearts.**

Leader: O Lord and Christ, you come disguised as the Christ of all children,

All: **yet we fail to find room for your manger in our crowded world.**

Leader: O overwhelming and empowering Spirit,
          you come breathing new life into our tired beings,

All: **yet we are content with our old selves and our worn-out ways.**

Leader: O come, Emmanuel, and set our feet again on Bethlehem's road.
          Open our ears to listen for angels' songs,
          our eyes to watch for celestial light,
          and our hearts to greet your presence.

All: **Amen.**

◆◆◆   3.2.5

The following resource for Christmas Eve worship combines gathering and penitential acts along with songs of praise. During the initial versicle, a Christ candle may be lighted. The refrain of the hymn is repeated as a doxology to conclude the act. The period of silence should be generous enough for individual meditation and confession.

Leader: The people who walked in darkness have seen a great light;
          those who dwelt in a land of deep darkness —
          on them has light shined.

All: **For a child has been born for us, a son given to us.**

Leader: Authority rests upon his shoulders,
          and his name will be called

All: **Wonderful Counselor,**
          Mighty God,
          Everlasting Father,
          Prince of Peace.   —Isaiah 9:2, 6

All may stand and sing: GLORIA

All: **Angels we have heard on high sweetly singing o'er the plains,**
          And the mountains in reply echoing their joyous strains.
          Gloria in excelsis Deo, Gloria in excelsis Deo!

          Shepherds, why this jubilee? Why your joyous strains prolong?
          What the gladsome tidings be which inspire your heav'nly song?
          Gloria in excelsis Deo, Gloria is excelsis Deo!

All: Something deep within us yearns to be born this night, O God —
               A deep yearning for a wholeness
                 to heal what seems to be torn apart
                 and to restore us to heaven's peace;
               A vast hope for a new kind of world
                 that is born not in the shouts of violence
                 but in the promise of the Prince of Peace;
               An ageless remembrance of an infant's cry
                 beckoning grownups to try to become children again;
               A bundle of emotions welling up from the depth of our being,
                 protesting their suppression, and seeking to find expression
                 in the intimacy of meaningful and lasting human relationships.
               O God of promise and fulfillment,
                 take us to Bethlehem, to the Place of Bread,
                 that this night our eyes may see your salvation,
                 and in seeing we may believe,
                 and that in believing we may find the One born tonight for us.

Silence

Solo: *Singing*   GLORIA
          Come to Bethlehem and see him whose birth the angels sing;
          Come, adore on bended knee Christ, the Lord, the newborn King.

All: *Singing*
          Gloria in excelsis Deo! Gloria in excelsis Deo!

◆◆◆ 3.2.6

In the following, the periods of silence should be sufficient for silent reflection. The leader simply needs to speak the sentences following the silences in a bidding voice, and the congregation will follow. There is no need for verbal rubrics. The concluding Gloria in excelsis is the refrain of the hymn "Angels We Have Heard on High" as set to the tune GLORIA. It may be sung with keyboard accompaniment or a cappella. Other settings of the Gloria in Excelsis may be found at numbers 3.3.9, 3.4.7, and 3.4.8.

Leader 1: Let us pray:

All: You are waiting to be found, O Christ,
               hidden amid the stuff that fills our mangers.
          You are waiting to be found, O Child of Peace,
               abandoned and abused by world now bent on war.
          We are searching for you, but we cannot find you,
               for our sin distorts our seeing and hearing.
          So, since we cannot find you on our own,
               find us in our groping, and take us safely in your arms
               to the places of refuge where you would have us go,
               that we may find the peace for which we so desperately yearn.

Lord, have mercy on us. *Silence.*
Christ, have mercy on us. *Silence.*
Lord, have mercy on us. *Silence.*

Leader 1: Listen again to the comforting assurance of the grace of God,
            promised in the Gospel to all who repent and believe:

Leader 2: "Do not be afraid; for see —
            I am bringing you good news of great joy for all the people:
            to you is born this day in the city of David a Savior,
            who is the Messiah, the Lord.
            This will be a sign for you:
            you will find a child wrapped in bands of cloth
            and lying in a manger."

Leader 1: And suddenly there was with the angel a multitude of the heavenly host,
            praising God and saying,

All: *Singing*
        Gloria in excelsis deo! Gloria in excelsis deo!   —Luke 2:10–13, adapt.

◆◆◆   3.2.7

In the following, the Kyrie *portion may be said or sung responsively. It is highly effective if the Leader 2 part is sung a cappella. The congregation repeats the same phrases singing either a cappella or with the keyboard accompaniment which may be found on page 205. Another variant is simply to speak the* Kyrie *portion in unison, omitting the repeated phrases.*

Leader 1: This is the message we have heard from God and proclaim to you:

Leader 2: God is light and in God there is no darkness at all.

Leader 1: If we say that we have fellowship with God
            while we are walking in darkness,
            we lie and do not do what is true;

Leader 2: but if we walk in the light, we have fellowship with one another,
            and the blood of Jesus cleanses us from all sin.

Leader 1: If we say that we have no sin, we deceive ourselves,
            and the truth is not in us.

Leader 2: but if we confess our sins,
            God who is faithful and just will forgive us our sins
            and cleanse us from all unrighteousness.   —1 John 1:5–9, adapt.

Leader 1: O God whose glory was shown at the beginning
            and shall be yet revealed,

All: **forgive us for blinding ourselves to the light of your creation,**
for dwelling in darkness and shadows,
and for our continual resistance to being changed
from glory into glory.

Leader 2: Lord, have mercy on us.

All:

Lord,   have   mer - cy   on   us.

Leader 1: O God whose glory was shown in the birth and resurrection
of your son, Jesus Christ,

All: **forgive our slowness to listen to him,**
our failure to know him,
our reluctance to follow him.

Leader 2: Christ, have mercy on us.

All:

Christ,   have   mer - cy   on   us.

Leader 1: O God whose glory was poured out upon your people
through the gifts of the Holy Spirit,

All: **forgive our insensitivity to the needs of other people,**
our inability to exercise the spiritual gifts,
our privacy of faith.

Leader 2: Lord, have mercy on us.

All:

Lord,   have   mer - cy   on   us.

Music: F. Russell Mitman © 2004

Leader 1: Listen to the comforting assurance of the grace of God,
promised in the Gospel to all who repent and believe:

Leader 2: Jesus said, "I am the light of the world.
Whoever follows me will never walk in darkness
but will have the light of life."   —John 8:35–36, adapt.

All: We believe the good news!
        Thanks be to God!

◆◆◆   3.2.8

*The following is designed for the Week of Prayer for Christian Unity or for any occasion when
the unity of the church is celebrated.*

Lord Jesus Christ, Head of the church,
    we gather this hour as a pilgrim people,
    searching for a wholeness that seems ever more remote.
We stand divided, our past loyalties blinding us
    to the needs and the realities of the present.
We find ourselves irreversibly entrenched in human rationales
    that continue to tear us farther apart.
Yet we dare to ask for your Holy Spirit to descend upon your church once more,
    to break down the barriers of division
    and to pull down the walls of separation.
Let us know how good and pleasant it is to dwell in unity,
    and be led on our road with the vision and the promise
    that one day your people may all be one.

◆◆◆   3.2.9

*The following penitential act begins with the singing of four stanzas of "O for a Closer Walk
with God." This hymn is sung to several tunes:* CAITHNESS, BEATITUDO, DALEHURST.

Hymn: *Please remain seated.*

O for a closer walk with God, a calm and heavenly frame,
a light to shine upon the road that leads us to the Lamb!

Where is the blessedness we knew when first our hearts were stirred?
Where is the soul-refreshing view of Jesus Christ, the Word?

Return, O holy Dove, return, sweet messenger of peace!
Forgive our sins and help us learn in Christ to find release.

The dearest idols we have known, as we our ways pursue;
help us to tear them from your throne, and worship only you.

                                        Words: William Cowper, 1772, alt.

Leader: Let us pray:

All: Holy God, we come into your presence with unclean lips,
               for we dwell in the midst of a world of unclean lips.
           We have missed the mark you intend for us,
               and sin of self and society clings to us so closely.

The idols of human making hold us captive,
   and we find ourselves in bondage to the forces of evil.

Silence

All: Tear us, O Lord, from the idols' grasp,
       and hold us in the arms of a grace bigger than our sin.
       for our strength is weak, and our power is frail.

Leader: Listen to the comforting assurance of the grace of God,
          promised in the Gospel to all who repent and believe:
          "God so loved the world that he gave his only Son,
          so that everyone who believes in him may not perish
          but may have eternal life."   —John 3:16
          Believe the good news: In Jesus Christ we are forgiven!

All: Thanks be to God!

       Singing
       So shall our walk be close with God, calm and serene our frame;
       So purer light shall mark the road that leads us to the Lamb.

◆◆◆   3.2.10

In the following the words of assurance are joined integrally with the prayer of confession. If this is used on Sundays on which the Hebrews text(s) are appointed or chosen, the worshipers will recognize how Scripture texts shape liturgical expressions. The prayer of confession is simultaneously a prayer for illumination. Hence, there is no need for another prayer for illumination before the Scripture readings.

Prayer of Confession: in unison

O God, whose Word has been since the beginning of creation:
   we confess our failure today to hear the voice of your prompting.
We have silenced the prophets' clarion calls
   and allowed the world's blaring noises to deafen us to your quiet whispers.
Yet deep inside us there is a silent emptiness that echoes our loneliness
   and cries out for a word to break the solitary stillness.
O God, we wait again for your Word.
Give us hearts of patience to listen for it and ears of courage to hear it.

Silence

Words of Assurance:

Leader 1:   "This is the covenant that I will make with them after those days," says the
            Lord: "I will put my laws in their hearts, and I will write them on their
            minds. . . . I will remember their sins no more."

Leader 2: Therefore, my friends, since we have confidence to enter the sanctuary by the new and living way that Christ opened for us, and since we have a great priest over the house of God, let us approach with a true heart in full assurance of faith, with our hearts sprinkled clean and our bodies washed with pure water. Let us hold fast to the confession of our hope without wavering, for the One who has promised is faithful.

—Hebrews 10:16–17, 19–23, adapt.

All: **We believe the Good News. In Jesus Christ we are forgiven.**

◆◆◆ 3.2.11

The following is designed for use on Ash Wednesday or on the First Sunday in Lent.

**Converting God, whose face is turned toward us in Jesus Christ:
we come this day/night to have our faces turned—
Turned from the ways, barren and desolate, on which we've spent our lives,
Turned away from the ways of self-gratification
and presumed self-sufficiency that have led us nowhere,
Turned to follow the path that leads to Jerusalem, to Gethsemane, to Golgotha,
and to Joseph's garden,
Turned to follow with Jesus the way of the cross,
that we may share also with Christ in the new life of Easter's dawn.**

Lord, have mercy on us! *Silence*

Christ, have mercy on us! *Silence*

Lord, have mercy on us! *Silence*

◆◆◆ 3.2.12

The following penitential act includes corresponding words of assurance. A Kyrie or the response Jesus, Lamb of God (music on page 212) may be sung following the period of silence.

Leader: At your name, O Jesus, every knee should bow in joyous worship,

All: **yet there is a certain pride that stands us stiff and unbending.**

Leader: Every tongue should declare your name above every name,

All: **but praise comes slowly to lips preoccupied with self-interests,
and reverence is rare in hearts set on self-sufficiency.**

Leader: In self-emptying love you humbled yourself for all humanity,
and took upon yourself the form of a slave for us,
becoming obedient even unto death on a cross.
Therefore you have given us a life-pattern for our following,
and a mold for modeling our ministry and mission.

All: Yet, our minds are set on the things that charm us most,
             and in our arrogance we even defend the negligence
               that glares at us in the mirrors of our souls.
             Lord Jesus Christ, our wrong cries out for a forgiveness
             bigger than our sin.

Please be seated or kneel in silence.

Leader: The saying is sure and worthy of full acceptance, that Christ Jesus came
             into the world to save sinners.   —1 Timothy 1:15

All: **Thanks be to God!**

◆◆◆ 3.2.13

Portions of Psalm 139 are appointed for a number of Sundays in the Revised Common Lectionary. *Since it is by nature a penitential psalm, it may be used as a prayer of confession and does not need necessarily to be read again as one of the Scripture lessons. Depending on which verses are appointed, the prayer may be adapted to include those verses. The response may be said or sung either a cappella or with the simple two-part accompaniment for keyboard or two instruments, which may be found on page 206. It also may be used as a congregational Psalter reading.*

Response:

O Lord, you have searched me and known me.
You know when I sit down and when I rise up;
you discern my thoughts from far away.
You search out my path and my lying down,
and are acquainted with all my ways.
Even before a word is on my tongue,
O Lord, you know it completely.
Such knowledge is too wonderful for me;
it is so high that I cannot attain it. *Response*

Where can I go from your spirit?
Or where can I flee from your presence?
If I ascend to heaven, you are there!
If I make my bed in Sheol, you are there!
If I take the wings of the morning
and settle at the farthest limits of the sea,

even there your hand shall lead me,
and your right hand shall hold me fast.   *Response.*

Search me, O God, and know my heart;
test me and know my thoughts.
See if there is any wicked way in me,
and lead me in the way everlasting.   *Response*

> Words: Psalm 139:1–4, 6–10, 23–24; music: F. Russell Mitman copyright © 2004

◆◆◆   3.2.14

In the following the Kyrie portion may be sung as printed, or it may be spoken as a continuation of the prayer of confession. In either case, there should be no gap between the sections. Suitable words of assurance may follow. The musical accompaniment may be found on page 206.

Holy God, before whom we stand in awe,
  we confess that we have missed the mark you intend for us.
We have yielded to the power of temptation
  and have overstepped the boundaries of our humanness.
We have disobeyed you and have neglected our neighbors.
We have ignored our holy calling and have misused the means of grace.
Our sin cries out for your forgiving touch!

> Music copyright © 1987 F. Russell Mitman

◆◆◆   3.2.15

Leader: O God who lavished on the world
            a love that gave up your only Son:

All: **We bow beneath his cross in the silent poverty of our sin.**

Please be seated or kneel in silent confession.

Leader: In the shadow of a love so amazingly steadfast
            and divinely generous:

All: We see the feebleness of our own devotion
             and the selfishness of our own desires.
         We have claimed an easy faith
             but denied a costly discipleship.
         We have been quick to judge the motives of others
             but slow to examine our own.
         We have been eager to point out the mote in the eye
             of our brother or sister,
         Yet we have been unaware of the log
             that blinds our own seeing the truth.
         We have justified a comfortable luxury for ourselves
             but have rationalized a stingy austerity for others.
         O God, we have received so much but given so little,
             and the double standards that have rent us asunder
             cry out for a healing forgiveness!

This may be followed with the singing of a Kyrie.

♦♦♦   3.2.16

Eternal God, we suffer from the sin of indecision.
You have made clear the way in Jesus Christ,
   yet we have avoided that way
   and have sought to justify our vacillation in endless rationales.
We have a way of making big things small and small things big.
O God, we are torn apart—knowing the way, yet wanting to avoid it.
By your mercy, shown fully in the passion and resurrection of Christ,
   forgive our indecision, and prod us again on the way to the cross,
   that when Easter dawns upon us,
   we may be reassured of your ageless decision for us. Amen.

♦♦♦   3.2.17

O Jesus, forgive our Palm Sunday parades:
   our noisy gongs and clanging cymbals,
   our martial drums and easy speeches!
Our vision is blinded by the thronging mob,
   our ears deafened by the shouting crowd,
   our minds distracted by the catchy cadences.

O Christ, forgive us for hiding behind our hurrahs.
Forgive us for forcing you to march to the beat of our own drums
   instead of receiving you hidden in the form of a servant.
Forgive us for catching only fleeting glimpses of you
   passing through the streets of our lives
   instead of meeting you and following you on your way.

O One who comes in the name of the Lord,
  forgive us, for we know not what we do!

◆◆◆ 3.2.18

The following penitential act is best used when communicants are seated at a table or tables, as is the custom frequently on Maundy Thursday. It may be prefaced by the reading of John 13:3–9. Through the pouring and splashing of the water in the bowl, the washing of the hands, and the touching of one another in the act of drying each other's hands, it seeks to involve the participants in a liturgical act that is more than words. The leader's readings are pluralized as corporate petitions while the congregation's lines are kept in the singular as individual confessions. Although this act is designed for use on Maundy Thursday, it need not be restricted to that observance.

Leader: Have mercy on us, O God, according to your steadfast love.

All: **According to your abundant mercy, blot out my transgressions.**

Leader: Wash us thoroughly from our iniquity, and cleanse us from our sin.

All: **For I know my transgressions, and my sin is ever before me.**

Leader: Against you, you alone, have we sinned, and done what is evil in your sight,

All: **Indeed, I was born guilty, a sinner when my mother conceived me.**

Leader: You desire truth in the inward being;

All: **therefore teach me wisdom in my secret heart.**

Leader: Purge us with hyssop, and we shall be clean;

All: **wash me, and I shall be purer than snow.**

The server pours water from a pitcher into a bowl; each person washes his or her hands as the bowl is passed, and the server dries each person's hands with a towel.

Leader: Create in us a clean heart, O God.

All: **And renew a right spirit within me.**

Leader: Do not cast us away from your presence,

All: **And do not take your holy spirit from me.**

Leader: Restore to us the joy of your salvation,

All: **And sustain in me a willing spirit.**

                                                              —Psalm 51:1–4a, 5–7, 10–12, adapt.

◆◆◆ 3.2.19

O God, we confess to you how slow we are
to hear, to see, to feel, to know, and to follow
the signs of Christ risen among us.
Pardon the sin of our disbelief,
and wash us thoroughly with regenerating grace,
that as we approach this meeting with him at this table,
we may be freed from our bondage to our self-determined barriers
and opened to receive the One who comes to make us and all things new. Amen.

◆◆◆ 3.2.20

The following act is most effective if done without announcements or directions. The leader may begin the unison prayer, and the congregation will follow. The hymn is generally set to the tunes REST *or* REPTON *(with last phrase repeated). The only musical introduction necessary is the last phrase. The time of silence should be sufficient for silent confession and meditation.*

Leader: To you, O Lord, I lift up my soul.

All: **O my God, in you I trust.**

Leader: Make me to know your ways, O Lord: teach me your paths.

All: **Lead me in your truth, and teach me,**
for you are the God of my salvation;
for you I wait all day long.

Leader: Be mindful of your mercy, O Lord, and of your steadfast love,
for they have been from of old.

All: **Do not remember the sins of my youth or my transgressions;**
according to your steadfast love remember me,
for your goodness' sake, O Lord!   —Psalm 25:1–2a, 4–7

All: *Singing*
Dear Lord and Father of mankind,
or **Dear God, embracing humankind,**
forgive our foolish ways.
Reclothe us in our rightful mind,
in purer lives your service find,
in deeper reverence, praise.

All: Most merciful God:
We have erred and strayed from your ways like lost sheep.
We have followed too much the devices and desires of our own hearts.
We have offended against your holy laws.
We have left undone those things which we ought to have done;

and we have done those things which we ought not to have done;
and there is no health in us.
Lord, have mercy on us.
Spare those who confess their faults.
Restore those who are penitent,
according to the promises you declared to all humankind
in Christ Jesus our Lord.
And grant, for his sake,
that we may hereafter live godly, righteous, and dedicated lives,
to the glory of your holy name. Amen.

           —Book of Common Prayer, alt.

All: *Singing*
    In simple trust like theirs who heard,
    beside the Syrian sea,
    the gracious calling of the Lord,
    let us, like them, without a word,
    rise up and followers be.

    Drop your still dews of quietness,
    till all our strivings cease;
    take from our souls the strain and stress,
    and let our ordered lives confess
    the beauty of your peace.

    Silence

    Breathe through the heats of our desire
    your coolness and your balm;
    let sense be dumb, let flesh retire;
    speak through the earthquake, wind, and fire,
    O still, small voice of calm.

◆◆◆ 3.2.21

The following is inspired by Jesus' parable of the prodigal son. "Parent God" may be substituted for "Our Father."

Our Father, we come before you today
 a fragmented and broken family.
We have gone our separate ways
 seeking meaning that becomes ever more elusive.
Searching for inner peace
 we have isolated ourselves from one another.
Yearning for independence we have denied our birthright,
 and have broken our relationships with you
 and with our brothers and sisters.

How alone we feel!
How afraid we are of the sights and sounds that surround us!
In the far country of our wanderings
   find us again and take us home. Amen.

◆◆◆   3.2.22

In the following, the Kyrie *portion may be sung. If so, let but a single note establish the pitch.*

Leader: Wondrous God,
         who sets suns and moons above us,
         mountains and valleys beneath us,
         and friends and strangers among us:

All: **How often have we tried to hide from your presence,**
         how seldom have we looked for your creating face
         and your fashioning hand!

         Lord, have mercy on us.

Leader: Wondrous God,
         who took upon yourself flesh of our flesh in Jesus our brother,
         and being found in human form
         made the ultimate disclosure of yourself in the face of Jesus Christ:

All: **How often we have forgotten you,**
         how seldom have we really loved and followed you!

         Christ, have mercy on us.

Leader: Wondrous God,
         who pours out freely the Holy Spirit:

All: **How often have we ignored your promptings,**
         how seldom have we asked for your help or accepted your gifts!

         Lord, have mercy upon us.

◆◆◆   3.2.23

Eternal God, who before the foundation of the world called us your own people
and in Christ Jesus promised to remain with us until the end of time,
we confess that the cares of the moment
have dulled our memory and have blinded our hope.
Forgive our preoccupation with the present,
and by your grace stretch the horizons of our minds,
that we may be given again the courage to remember and to hope. Amen.

◆◆◆ 3.2.24

Gracious God, who pours out freely the gift of your Holy Spirit:
   we confess before you and to each other
   that we have failed to recognize this most precious gift.
We have been satisfied with ordinary things,
   suspicious of different things,
   and blind to spiritual things.
Cleanse us, O God, with your celestial fire.
Burn away our presumptuous self-sufficiency,
   and open us in faith to receive the Spirit's renewing power. Amen.

◆◆◆ 3.2.25

Leader: O Creator God, by whose hand we are made
         and in whose hand we are held,

All: **how feeble is our faith and in your loving kindness,**
     how wavering our trust in your sovereignty over all!

Leader: O Christ, through whose pierced hands and side
         we are set free from bondage to sin and death,

All: **how slow are we to believe news almost too good to be true,**
     how unable to share it with others!

Leader: O Holy Spirit, whose commissioning power is handed over to us,

All: **how afraid we are to accept the call to righteousness,**
     how ashamed of holiness!

Leader: O holy and undivided Trinity, One God,

All: **have mercy on us, pardon our sin, and grant us your peace.**
     Amen.

◆◆◆ 3.2.26

O God whose parenting love over and around us lies,
how often we have wandered away from you.
Like a child alone in the crowd, we feel lost and forgotten.
Nevertheless, O God, we are reminded where we belong and to whom we belong.
So take us back again, through the love of your Son, Jesus Christ. Amen.

◆◆◆ 3.2.27

The following is shaped by the biblical stories of the Garden of Eden and the prodigal son.

Lord God, we hear you walking among us.
Your presence is inescapable.
Yet we feel ashamed and afraid.
Guilt gnaws away at our inner being, and we try to hide from you.
We have tried to make it alone and have trusted in the things we have made.
But something seems missing, and our idols have betrayed us.
Lord, find us in our secret hiding places with a love that will not let us go.
Find us in the far country of our exile with a grace that covers all our sin.
Find us in the clutter of our graven images with the truth that will set us free.

◆◆◆ 3.2.28

Leader: Lord, help us to become children,

All: **for our yearning to become unchildlike
has hindered us from entering into your realm.**

Leader: Lord, help us to become children,

All: **for in seeking self-discovery
we have blinded ourselves from the truth about ourselves.**

Leader: Lord, help us to become children,

All: **for in our search to understand reality
we have lost the power of imagination
you have given us to make our lives real.**

Leader: Lord, help us to become children,

All: **for in searching frantically for happiness and security
we have forgotten the spontaneity of joy, the fun of laughter,
and the meaning of surprise.**

Leader: Lord, help us to become children,

All: **for in rationalizing the unexplainable
we have missed the mystery and the awesomeness of realities
that lie beyond the grasp of our minds.**

Leader: Lord, help us to become children,

All: **for in wanting to put away childish things
we have rejected your Christ who comes as a child
to make us children again.**

◆◆◆   3.2.29

The following is designed for use in an outdoor worship setting. If appropriate, sufficient time should be given during the period of silence for the sounds of nature to be heard. A wordless assurance comes through the silence! The leader may wish also to provide brief pauses between each of the petitions.

Leader: Creator, when we bow our heads low to the ground
to keep our feet from faltering,

All: lift them up to sky, that the sun of your love may shine on our faces.

Leader: Creator, when our lips are too heavy from the burdens of the day
to sing you psalms of praise,

**All: open them up, that like a bird at daybreak
we may sing to you a new song.**

Leader: Creator, when our eyes are focused inward
in preoccupation with ourselves,

**All: turn them out and
lift them up to the hills,**
or   **stretch them across the plains,**
or   **extend them to the far horizons
that we may see the breadth and length and height and depth
of your care for us and all creation.**

Leader: Creator, when our minds are closeted and stale,

**All: blow them open with the wind of your Spirit,
that we may be filled with the freshness of your grace.**

Leader: Creator, when our bodies are hot from running
our feverish races for recognition

**All: pour over us the cooling waters
that bathe us with your accepting forgiveness.**

Leader: Creator, when our ears are deafened
by the beating of all the noisy drums in the streets of our lives,

**All: attune us again to the music of the earth
and the peaceful sounds of silence.**

Silence

The congregation may sing one or more stanzas of "For the Beauty of the Earth" as a thanksgiving response.

◆◆◆   3.2.30

Forgive, O God, our constant demanding:
    demanding of ourselves more than we have the right to expect,
    demanding of others a perfection we ourselves cannot attain,
    demanding of you the fulfillment of our every whim and desire.
Reclothe us in our rightful minds:
    to see ourselves as we really are — fallible and fragile,
    to find others as they are — imperfect and human,
    to know you as you are, O God,
        forgiving when we cannot forgive,
        accepting when we cannot accept,
        and loving when we cannot love.

◆◆◆   3.2.31

The following is an adaptation of Psalm 130. The last section, spoken by the leader, serves as the words of assurance. It may be followed immediately by an act of praise.

All: Out of the depths I cry to you, O Lord,
            Lord, hear my voice!
            Let your ears be attentive
            to the voice of my supplications!

Leader: If you, O Lord, should mark iniquities,
            who would survive?
            But there is forgiveness with you,
            so that you may be revered.

All: I wait for you, O Lord, my soul waits,
            and in your word I hope.
            My soul is longing for you, O Lord,
            more than those who watch for the morning.

Leader: With the Lord there is steadfast love
            and great power to redeem.
            God will redeem us from all our iniquities.   — Psalm 139:1–8, adapt.

◆◆◆   3.2.32

Leader: Let us pray.

All: Morning's praises come slow to our lips, O God,
                for the night's darkness lingers long in our lives.
            Thanksgiving is not natural for us,
                for complaints come easier than affirmations.

> Bring us, O God, from night into day:
>> from despairing over what life has dealt us
>>> into dependence on you for what life can be,
>> from rationalizations that excuse our sins of omission
>>> into the freedom for commission
>>> to follow the call of Christ,
>> from the lethargy that wants to keep us sleeping in the past
>>> into the courage that awakens us to your future.

Leader: Rise up, O Lord! Do not let mortals prevail;
            let the nations be judged before you.
         Put them in fear, O Lord;
            let the nations know that they are only human.

—Psalm 9:19–20

◆◆◆   3.2.33

We come into your presence, O Holy One,
   dragging on our feet the mire of everything profane
     in which we have found ourselves stuck.
We have not taken off the shoes of the world
   you have commanded us to shed as we stand here on holy ground.
So here we are, cloaked in the rags of our riches,
   unwashed, unworthy, unprepared for this divine encounter.
We beg you to take us as we are
   and to transform us into what you want us to be.
Wash us again in the grace left over from our baptism,
   and feed us with more than the bread we can buy:
     that when this time in your house is over today,
   we may find ourselves having been immersed in a splendor
     not of our making
   and enveloped in a glory beyond our imagining.
O One who is all in all, we stand in your house empty-handed,
   waiting for your presence in sacred silence.

Silence

◆◆◆   3.2.34

Leader: In a time when visions seem few, O God,
             and hopelessness captures many,
         we search for a sacred purpose for our lives
            and we yearn for a holy presence in our world.

All: **But why, O Lord, do you seem so far from us?**
         Destruction and violence flourish all around,
         strife and contention arise at every turn,

and bad things happen to good people.
Why do you not seem to listen when we cry to you for help,
why does your voice seem silenced?
We keep watch looking for a sign of a plan for us
and for a vision for our world.
Grant us patience, O God, to wait for you,
and your faithfulness to see us through tough times.

◆◆◆ 3.2.35

Leader: Let us throw off every encumbrance,
every sin which all too readily distracts us,
and look to Jesus who, for the sake of the joy that lay ahead of him,
endured the cross and its disgrace,
and is seated at the right hand of God.   —Hebrews 12:1b, 2b, adapt.

All: Lord Jesus, on whom our faith depends from beginning to end:
We find ourselves entered in a race for life.
Some of us, we admit, are slow at starting,
   unaware of life's purpose,
   and apathetic toward the goal of the race.
Some of us are too timid to run,
   anxious about whether we have the endurance,
   and afraid of the unexpected that might lie ahead.
Some of us are too angry to run,
   embittered over past losses, mad when life isn't fair,
   and alienated by conflict and competition.
Some of us are too tired to take one more step,
   exhausted by expectations and demands,
   and so weary of running for our lives.
Lord Jesus, when our knees go limp
   and our spirits faint:
Let us fall into the arms of a grace
   waiting by the road to refresh and to revive us.
And, while all of heaven cheers, keep pointing us
   to the race's end and the victor's prize. Amen.

Leader: Have you not known? Have you not heard?
The Lord, the everlasting God, the Creator of the ends of the earth,
does not faint or grow weary.

All: Those who wait for the Lord shall renew their strength,
they shall mount up with wings like eagles,
they shall run and not be weary,
they shall walk and not faint.   —Isaiah 40:28, 31, adapt.

This may be followed immediately by the singing of a doxology or other hymn of praise.

◆◆◆   3.2.36

O God of new starts and fresh beginnings,
   we come to you today burdened with the past's leftovers.
We feel guilty over the things we have left unfinished
   and the things we intended to start
      but never got around to doing.
We have grieved over life's little losses
   but have failed to search for the big finds.
We would rather be obsessed by what has passed us by
   than rejoice in what lies ahead.
Come after us in our wanderings, O God,
   like a shepherd hunting for a lost sheep,
   like a woman sweeping the house for a missing coin.
Find us in our lostness, and wrap us in an extravagant grace
   that lifts us on your shoulders
      and takes us home where we belong. Amen.

◆◆◆   3.2.37

It is so easy for us to forget you, O God,
   so easy to forget to be faithful.
Like a caring mother teaching her daughter to walk,
   you take us into your arms.
Like a devoted father keeping the reins on his son,
   you harness us in your love.
Like a protecting guardian fulfilling a child's every need,
   you stoop down and feed us.
Yet it is so easy for us to forget your parenting care,
   and there is something in us that is bent on turning from you
      to the lesser things that command our devotion.
Our unfaithfulness deserves your anger,
   yet your compassion for us grows ever more warm and tender.
So take us back again, O God, into the intimacy of your family,
   channel our infidel ways into an obedient faithfulness,
      and embrace us with a love that will never let go again. Amen.

◆◆◆   3.2.38

In the following the prayer of confession is joined with corresponding words of assurance.

All: God, whose Word has been since the beginning of creation:
            we confess our failure to hear the voice of your prompting today.
        We have silenced the prophets' clarion calls
           and allowed the world's blaring noises
              to deafen us to your quiet whispers.

Yet, deep inside us there is a silent emptiness
   that echoes our loneliness
      and cries out for a word to break the solitary stillness.
O God, we wait again for your word of reconciliation.
Give us the patience to listen for it
   and the courage to follow it.

Silence

Leader: Hear the word of God through the prophet Malachi:
       "For you who revere my name
       the sun of righteousness shall rise, with healing in its wings,
       and you shall go out leaping like calves from the stall."

                                —Malachi 4:5–6

All: **We believe the good news.**
        In Jesus Christ we are forgiven.

◆◆◆   3.2.39

As a gracious host, O God, you have prepared a table before us,
   and you have invited us to the wedding banquet.
Yet we acknowledge around your table
   that we have not always honored all people.
We have picked out those to whom we give preferential treatment
   that we might receive something special from them in return.
We have looked up to the famous and influential
   and have looked down on the marginalized and powerless.
At your table wait on us with a grace, O God,
   that forgives a past when our hospitality has been exclusive,
      and promises a future when all people
         will find a place of honor at your table.
Give us the humble courage to accept your invitation
   that we may find ourselves in communion
      with those we would fail to invite
         yet who will bless us with more than we can imagine. Amen.

◆◆◆   3.2.40

Leader: In the presence of God's holy splendor
       our humanness trembles in sacred awe.
       Therefore, let us come before the Holy One,
       acknowledging our sin and asking for God's forgiving grace.

All: **Holy God, into whose presence we come bearing the sins of our souls,**
        we confess our complicity in the world's idol-making.

The gods of culture and commerce have captured our imaginations,
    and we have offered them the glory that rightfully is yours.
As the cash registers rasp loudly their receipts,
    we feel robbed of the silent signature that marks our belonging.
O God, there is a great secular emptiness in us
    that cries out for a sacred touch!

Silence

Leader 1: Listen to the comforting assurance of the grace of God,
            promised in the Gospel to all who repent and believe:

Leader 2: "Thus says the Lord God:
            'I the Lord will answer those who come with the multitude of their idols,
            in order that I may take hold of their hearts,
            all of whom are estranged from me through their idols.'"
                                        —Ezekiel 14:4b–5, adapt.

            "Peace I leave with you; my peace I give to you.
            I do not give to you as the world gives.
            Do not let your hearts be troubled, and do not let them be afraid."
                                          —John 14:17

All: We believe the good news! Thanks be to God!

◆◆◆   3.2.41

The following is designed for use on World Communion Sunday.

Almighty God, Sovereign over all Creation,
    we gather as your church, holy and one
        throughout the whole wide earth,
We rejoice in your calling us to this table
    in the household of faith, east and west, north and south.
Yet, gathered around this table
    we also are reminded of the bitterness that tarnishes our holiness
    and the dividedness that threatens our oneness.
We acknowledge the seemingly insurmountable walls
    that separate east from west, north from south.
Yet also, by your promises made known to us in Jesus our Lord,
    we dare to ask for forgiveness and healing;
    we yearn to be made holy and one again;
    we dream of one communion of love throughout the whole wide earth;
    and we pray, with your Son, that his body someday may all be one.

◆◆◆ 3.2.42

The following combines a prayer of confession and words of assurance. It is especially appropriate for those Sundays when verses of Romans 5 are appointed in the Revised Common Lectionary *as the Epistle Lesson. This Scripture passage may be read by a second reader who is seated or is standing at a distance from the worship leader.*

Leader: O righteous and compassionate God,

All: We come to you as a church in a world numbed by fear.
   The threats of terrorism and the prospect of further violence
       paralyze us in our mission and ministry.
   We have withdrawn ourselves
       behind the defenses of militant nationalisms,
   and rationalized isolations
       that increasingly separate us from those with whom
           we share your precious creation.
   O God, we are so afraid, and we confess
       we have become addicted to an anesthetizing doubt
           that even you have no power to intervene
           in the chaos we mortals have wrought.
   We have sinned,
       we have grievously sinned against heaven and earth.
   We have left undone those things which we ought to have done,
       and we have done those things which we ought not to have done,
           and there is no wholeness in us.
   Lord, have mercy on us.

Silence

Leader: By your Holy Spirit,

All: Work again in us a wholehearted trust
       that enables us no longer to be conformed to this world
           but to be confirmed in the way that brings health and peace;
               through Jesus Christ our Lord. Amen.

◆◆◆ 3.2.43

The following prayer is shaped by Psalm 23, and the final sentence echoes the words of Isaac Watts's paraphrase of this Psalm in the hymn "My Shepherd Will Supply My Need."

Shepherd God, we stumble into your presence
   suffering from a great amnesia.
We seem abandoned, we feel forgotten, and we are prone to forgetting.
Forgive our aimless wanderings,
   our purposeless pastimes,
   our consuming emptiness.

O Love that will not let us go,
  break through the barriers of isolation
  and the layers of insulation that surround us.
Find us in our distant exile, and by your grace assure us
  that we are no longer strangers in your presence,
  nor mere guests in your house,
  but your own children at home. Amen.

◆◆◆ 3.2.44

This prayer is a companion to another Watts hymn "O God, Our Help in Ages Past." It is also appropriate for a funeral or memorial service. In some traditions the last Sunday of the church year is also a time of remembrance for all who have died during the time from Advent to Christ the King.

Eternal God, in whose sight a thousand ages are like an evening gone,
  we come to this hour bewildered by the shadows time casts over us.
Forgive us our unceasing dissatisfaction with the ever-rolling stream of time
  that is never fast enough or slow enough for us.
Forgive our slavish counting
  of the moments and hours and days and years that clock our lives.
Forgive our failure to see in the midst of the shadows of time
  the shadow-less grace in which we were conceived,
  and the timeless eternity to which we are destined.
And grant, O God,
  that within the swing of the pendulum that measures our lives
  we may be found responsive to the Christ who calls us now
  to the living of these days. Amen.

◆◆◆ 3.2.45

The following is designed for All Saints' Day/Sunday. The biblical images are those of Revelation and Psalm 91.

Leader 1: We stand before the Lamb who takes away the sin of the world,
       and our own humanness is bared, our own mortality exposed.

Leader 2: Come, then, let us approach the throne of grace,
       let us draw near with a true heart,
       that we may be cleansed of all uncleanness and made pure before God.

All: We humble ourselves in your divine presence, O Christ,
       uncomfortably aware of something in us
         that seems just a bit too tainted
         to abide in the shadow of the Almighty.
       We know not what it is that separates us from you and from others,
         yet we feel estranged, alienated, isolated, alone.

We remember all who have been sainted for their service,
yet our own witness sometimes seems so meager,
so meaningless, so trivial.

Silence may be observed, or the congregation or a choir may sing a setting of the Agnus Dei ("Lamb of God").

All: Purify us, by the inspiration of your Holy Spirit,
from all inward uncleanness,
and make us able and willing to serve you in newness of life,
to the glory of your Holy Name. Amen.

Silence

Leader 1:   Listen to the comforting assurance of the grace of God,
promised in the Gospel to all who repent and believe:

Leader 2:   "God so loved the world that he gave his only Son,
so that everyone who believes in him
may not perish but may have eternal life."   —John 3:16

Leader 1:   Believe the good news! In Jesus Christ you/we are forgiven!

All: Amen!
Blessing and glory and wisdom and thanksgiving and honor
and power and might be to our God forever and ever! Amen.
     —Revelation 7:12

WORDS OF ASSURANCE _____

◆◆◆   3.3.1

Leader: "Comfort my people," says our God. "Comfort them!
Encourage the people of Jerusalem.
Tell them they have suffered long enough,
and their sins are forgiven."   —Isaiah 40:1–2, TEV

All: Amen! Come, Lord Jesus!

◆◆◆   3.3.2

Leader: The Word became flesh and lived among us,

All: and we have seen his glory,
the glory as of a father's only son,
full of grace and truth.   —John 1:14

Unison: *Speaking*
Glory to God in the highest, and on earth peace, goodwill to all.

or

Sung to the refrain of "Angels We Have Heard on High"
Gloria in excelsis Deo! Gloria in excelsis Deo!

◆◆◆ 3.3.3

Leader 1: This is the message we have heard from God and proclaim to you:

Leader 2: God is light and in God there is no darkness at all.

All: If we walk in the light, we have fellowship with one another,
and the blood of Jesus Christ cleanses us from sin.

—1 John 1:5, 7, adapt.

◆◆◆ 3.3.4

In the following the words of Genesis are effective if spoken by a woman's voice. The response is sung to the tune STUTTGART.

Leader 1: Hear now the promise of God to Noah and his descendants,
even to endless generations:

Leader 2: "I have set my bow in the clouds,
and it shall be a sign of the covenant between me and the earth.
When I bring clouds over the earth and the bow is seen in the clouds,
I will remember my covenant that is between me and you
and every living creature." —Genesis 9:13–15

All: *Singing* STUTTGART
Far as east from west is distant, God has put away our sin;
Like the pity of a father has the Lord's compassion been.

As it was without beginning, so it lasts without end;
To their children's children ever shall God's righteousness extend.

◆◆◆ 3.3.5

Leader: Be assured that the grace of our Lord overflows for us
with the faith and love that are in Christ Jesus.
The saying is sure and worthy of full acceptance,
that Christ Jesus came into the world to save sinners.

All: To the Sovereign of the ages, immortal, invisible, the only God,
be honor and glory for ever and ever. Amen.

—1 Timothy 1:14–15, 17, adapt.

This may be followed immediately with the singing of a doxology or the hymn "Immortal, Invisible, God Only Wise."

◆◆◆   3.3.6

Here is another variant of the same text from 1 Timothy coupled with words of assurance
from one of John Calvin's liturgies.

Leader: The saying is sure and worthy of full acceptance,
          that Christ Jesus came into the world to save sinners.   — 1 Timothy 1:15

          Let us believe therefore,
          that when we ask God's mercy in the name of our Lord Jesus,
          and when we sincerely forgive our neighbors,
          our Lord forgives us, and through the faith we have in Jesus Christ
          our hearts are cleansed.
                              — from John Calvin, "The Form of Church Prayers," adapt.

◆◆◆   3.3.7

Leader: Behold the Lamb of God who takes away the sin of the world!
          He was despised and rejected by mortals;
          a man of sorrows and acquainted with grief.

All: **Surely he has borne our griefs and carried our sorrows.**

Leader: He was wounded for our transgressions,
          he was bruised for our iniquities;

All: **Upon him was the punishment that made us whole,**
          and by his bruises we are healed.
                              — John 1:29, Isaiah 53:3–5, RSV and NRSV, adapt.

◆◆◆   3.3.8

Leader: God shows divine love toward us,
          in that while we were still sinners, Christ died for us.

All: *Singing*   HAMBURG
          Were the whole realm of nature mine,
          that were a present far too small;
          Love so amazing, so divine,
          demands my soul, my life, my all. Amen.
                                          Words: Isaac Watts, 1707, alt.

◆◆◆   3.3.9

The leader in the following may speak both parts. The praise response is the ancient Gloria
in Excelsis, *as translated by the ecumenical Consultation on Common Texts. It may be sung*
or said in unison. An alternative is the translation of Nikolaus Decius's metrical setting of
the Gloria in Excelsis, *"All Glory Be to God on High." Another translation is the one by*

F. Bland Tucker. In many hymnals it is set to the tune, ALLEIN GOTT IN DER HÖH' SEI EHR *that Decius composed for his German paraphrase of the ancient Latin text. It also may be sung to* MIT FREUDEN ZART.

Leader 1: Listen to the comforting assurance of the grace of God,
              promised in the Gospel to all who repent and believe:

Leader 2: "God so loved the world that he gave his only Son,
              that everyone who believes in him may not perish but have eternal life.
              Indeed, God did not send the Son into the world to condemn the world,
              but in order that the world might be saved through him."
                                        —John 3:16–17

Leader 1: Believe the good news that in Jesus Christ we are forgiven!

Leader 2: O Lord, open our lips!

All: **And our mouths shall show forth your praise!**

All: *Singing or speaking*
Glory to God in heaven,
    peace and grace to his people on earth.
We praise you for your great glory,
    we worship you, we give you thanks,
Lord God, heavenly King, Almighty God and Father.

Lord Jesus Christ, Lamb of God, only Son of the Father,
    you take away the sin of the world, have mercy on us.
You sit at the right hand of the Father, hear our prayer.
You alone are the Holy One, you alone are the Lord,
    you alone are the Most High, Jesus Christ, with the Holy Spirit,
    in the glory of the Father.
Amen.

or

All: **All glory be to God on high and thanks for all God's mercy.**
To us no harm shall e'er come nigh, now and to all eternity.
God takes delight in humankind,
and peace in us its home shall find,
all warfare now is ended.

We praise, we worship you, we trust, and give you thanks forever.
O God, your rule is right and just, and wise, and changes never.
Your boundless power o'er all things reigns,
You do whate'er your will ordains;
'Tis well you are our ruler.

O Jesus Christ, our God and Lord, begotten of the Father.
O you who have our peace restored, and the lost sheep shall gather.

O Lamb of God enthroned on high,
behold our need and hear our cry!
Have mercy on us, Jesus!

O Holy Spirit, precious gift, O comforter unfailing,
From evil's power our souls uplift against the foe prevailing.
Avert our woes and calm our dread;
for us the Savior's blood was shed;
O God, in faith sustain us!

Words: Nikolaus Decius, 1526; stanza 1 trans. F. Russell Mitman, 2004;
stanzas 2–4 trans. Catherine Winkworth, 1862, alt.

◆◆◆ 3.3.10

Another variant of John 3:16–17 is in the following. The biblical text may be spoken by a second leader at some distance from the first one. Shouting, the Psalms tell us, is an appropriate liturgical response!

Leader: Listen to the comforting assurance of the grace of God, promised in the Gospel to all who repent and believe:

God so loved the world that he gave his only Son, so that everyone who believes in him may not perish but may have eternal life. Indeed, God did not send the Son into the world to condemn the world, but in order that the world might be saved through him. — John 3:16–17

Sisters and brothers, believe the Good news!
In Jesus Christ we are forgiven!

All: *Shouting*
Amen! Hallelujah!

◆◆◆ 3.3.11

Leader: Before the foundation of the world God chose us in Christ
to become holy and blameless, destining us, by God's own purpose
for adoption as God's children through Jesus Christ.

All: Praise the glorious grace
that God freely bestowed on us in the Beloved!

Leader: In Christ we are redeemed,
and have received the forgiveness of our sins
through the abundant grace lavished on us. — Ephesians 1:4–8, adapt.

All: *Singing* LASST US ERFREUEN
From all who dwell below the skies let the Creator's praise arise;
Alleluia! Alleluia!
Let the Redeemer's name be sung through ev'ry land, by ev'ry tongue.
Alleluia! Alleluia! Alleluia! Alleluia! Alleluia!

Words: Isaac Watts, 1719

◆◆◆ 3.3.12

Leader: Whoever is in Christ is a new creation;
everything old has passed away, behold, everything has become new!

All: **All this is from God who reconciled us through Christ**
and gave us the ministry of reconciliation.
—2 Corinthians 5:17–18, adapt.

Leader: Once we were no people!

All: **Now we are God's people!** —1 Peter 2:10, adapt.

All: *Singing* NEW BRITAIN
Amazing grace! how sweet the sound that saved a wretch like me!
I once was lost, but now am found, was blind, but now I see.
Words: John Newton, 1779

◆◆◆ 3.3.13

In the following, the response, inspired by images in the letter to the Ephesians and the first letter of Peter may be sung to WESTMINSTER ABBEY *or* REGENT SQUARE.

Leader: Now in Christ Jesus you who once were far off
have been brought near by the blood of Christ.

All: **For Christ is our peace.**

Leader: So then you are no longer strangers and aliens,
but you are citizens with the saints
and also members of the household of God,
built upon the foundation of the apostles and prophets,
with Christ Jesus himself as the cornerstone.

All: **In Christ the whole structure is joined together**
and grows into a holy temple,
in whom we are built together spiritually
into a dwelling place for God. —Ephesians 2:13–14, 19–22, adapt.

Response: **Christ is made the sure foundation,**
Christ the head and cornerstone,
chosen of our God, and precious,
binding all the church in one,
building living stones together,
for a house to be God's own.
Words: seventh-century Latin hymn, trans. John Mason Neale, 1851, alt.

◆◆◆   3.3.14

Leader: Jesus promised:
          "Ask, and it will be given you; search and you will find;
          knock, and the door will be opened for you."   —Matthew 7:7
          Therefore, I announce that in Jesus Christ you/we are forgiven.

All: Amen.

◆◆◆   3.3.15

Leader: The Lord is merciful and gracious,
          slow to anger and abounding in steadfast love.
          God does not deal with us according to our sins,
          nor repay us according to our iniquities.
          For as the heavens are high above the earth,
          so great is the Lord's steadfast love toward those
          who have reverence for God.
                                              —Psalm 103:8, 10–11, alt.

All: **As far as the east is from the west,
          so far God removes our transgressions from us.**
                                              —Psalm 103:12, alt.

or

All: *Singing*   STUTTGART
          **Far as east from west is distant,
          God has put away our sin;
          Like the pity of a father
          has the Lord's compassion been.**

And with either:

          **O my soul, bless your Redeemer;
          All within me, bless God's name;
          Bless the Savior, and forget not
          all God's mercies to proclaim.**
                              Hymn stanzas: from *The Book of Psalms*, 1871, alt.

◆◆◆   3.3.16

Leader 1: Believe the good news:

Leader 2: "If anyone sins, we have an advocate, Jesus Christ the righteous,
          who is the atoning sacrifice for our sins, and not for ours only
          but also for the sins of the whole world."   —1 John 1:1b–2, adapt.

All: **In Jesus Christ we are forgiven.**

◆◆◆ 3.3.17

Leader: The Lord is gracious and merciful,

All: **forbearing and abounding in steadfast love.**

Leader: The Lord is good to all,

All: **and has compassion over all creation.**

Leader: The Lord's words are faithful.

All: **The Lord's deeds are gracious.**

Leader: The Lord's ways are just.

All: **The Lord's doings are kind.**

Leader: My mouth will speak the praise of the Lord,

All: **and all people will bless God's holy name forever.**
> —Psalm 145:8–9, 13b, 17, 21, adapt.

◆◆◆ 3.3.18

Leader: God who is rich in mercy, out of great love for us,
even when we were dead in our disobedience,
made us alive together with Christ,
raised us up with him,
and seated us with him in the heavenly places.
For, it is by grace you have been saved through faith,
and this is not your own doing,
it is the gift of God.   —Ephesians 2:4–6, 8, adapt.

All: **Thanks be to God!**

This may be followed with the singing of a doxology or hymn of thanksgiving.

◆◆◆ 3.3.19

Leader: Since we are justified by faith,
we have peace with God through our Lord Jesus Christ.

All: **Through Christ we have obtained access**
to this grace in which we stand,
and we rejoice in our hope of sharing the glory of God.
> —Romans 5:1–2

PRAISE RESPONSES _____

The corporate praises of Israel were the Psalms. They also found their way into the liturgical expressions of the early church and got a fresh revitalization as corporate praise during the Reformation of the sixteenth century. In the structure of the liturgy, in addition to their use as "graduals" between Old Testament and New Testament reading, another place for the reading or singing of Psalms is as a praise response to the assurance of God's forgiveness. Since the Psalms are essentially songs, it is entirely appropriate for them to be sung either as canticles or, as was the preference of Reformed churches, in metrical form. It is traditional for the Trinitarian Gloria Patri ("Glory to the Father") to be appended.

Many settings of the texts and tunes for the corporate singing and speaking of the Psalms exist. They cannot be reproduced here, and thus I refer the reader to the many other sources, both ancient and modern.

Besides the sung or spoken acts of praise accompanying some of the resources in the previous section of this chapter, additional praise expressions are included here. Most of the calls to praise that are part of those acts are interchangeable with the ones included here.

◆◆◆ 3.4.1

Leader: Praise the Lord, O my soul!

All: And all that is in me, praise God's holy name!   —Psalm 103:1, adapt.

◆◆◆ 3.4.2

Leader: Lift up your voices in praise!

◆◆◆ 3.4.3

Leader: Lift up your hearts!

All: Let God be praised!

◆◆◆ 3.4.4

Leader: O God, open our lips!

All: And our mouths shall speak out your praise!   —Psalm 51:15, alt.

◆◆◆ 3.4.5

The following praise response for Advent may be sung to any of several tunes, the most familiar of which are STUTTGART, IN BABILONE, *and* HYFRYDOL *(two stanzas joined together).*

Come, thou long-expected Jesus, born to set thy people free;
From our fears and sins release us, let us find our rest in thee.

Born thy people to deliver, born a child and yet a King.
Born to reign in us forever, now thy gracious kingdom bring.

Words: Charles Wesley, 1744

◆◆◆ 3.4.6

The following is the nineteenth-century translation of Philipp Nicolai's hymn by Catherine Winkworth, alt. A contemporary translation has been prepared by Carl P. Daw Jr., and still another appears in the Lutheran Book of Worship. *The tune is* WACHET AUF. *The hymn generally appears in the Advent section of most hymnals. However, it also may be used on All Saints' Day/Sunday or in a funeral or memorial service.*

Now let all the heavens adore thee,
and saints and angels sing before thee.
With harp and cymbal's clearest tone;
Of one pearl each shining portal,
where we shall join the choirs immortal
in praises round thy glorious throne.
No vision ever brought,
no ear hath ever caught such great glory!
Therefore will we, eternally,
sing hymns of joy and praise to thee.

◆◆◆ 3.4.7

The following is the last stanza of the familiar hymn "While Shepherds Watched Their Flocks by Night" by Nahum Tate. It is generally viewed as a Christmas hymn, especially when wedded to George Frederick Handel's music, the tune of which is named CHRISTMAS. *However, it may be substituted as well for the* Gloria in Excelsis *on other occasions throughout the church year. And it may be sung to other common meter tunes such as* WINCHESTER OLD, ST. COLUMBA, *and the lively* MCKEE.

All glory be to God on high, and to the earth be peace;
Goodwill to all from highest heaven begin and never cease.

Words: Nahum Tate, 1700, alt.

◆◆◆ 3.4.8

Leader: Glory to God in the highest!

All: **And peace on earth.**

Unison: *Singing, to the refrain of "Angels We Have Heard on High"*
Gloria in excelsis deo!
Gloria in excelsis deo!

◆◆◆ 3.4.9

The following praise response is one of a number of stanzas of an anonymous eighteenth-century German hymn that was translated in the nineteenth century by Edward Caswell and others. It begins with the words, "When morning gilds the skies, my heart, awakening cries, 'May Jesus Christ be praised!'" The opening stanzas may be sung as a gathering hymn, this one as a praise response, and the final one, "Be this, while life is mine, my canticle divine..." as a sending hymn. The tune most wedded to these words is Joseph Barnby's LAUDES DOMINI.

To God, the Word, on high, the hosts of angels cry;
   May Jesus Christ be praised!
Let mortals, too, upraise their voice in hymns of praise:
   May Jesus Christ be praised!

Words: Edward Caswell, 1849, and others

◆◆◆ 3.4.10

Suggested tunes for the following are REGENT SQUARE, ST. PETER'S WESTMINSTER, *or* LAUDA ANIMA.

Glory be to Christ who loved us, washed us from each spot and stain;
Glory be to Christ who bought us, paid the price our souls to gain;
Glory, glory, glory, glory to the Lamb who once was slain.

Words: Horatius Bonar (1808–1889), alt.

◆◆◆ 3.4.11

The following is a joyous doxology for Trinity Sunday or other occasions. Suggested tunes are HYFRYDOL, BEACH SPRING, *or* NETTLETON.

Alleluia! Alleluia! Glory be to God on high;
Alleluia to the Savior who has won the victory;
Alleluia to the Spirit, fount of love and sanctity;
Alleluia! Alleluia! to the triune majesty!

Words: Christopher Wordsworth, 1872

◆◆◆ 3.4.12

The book of Revelation in the Bible contains many songs and other liturgical expressions of the early church. The following, with several options, is designed for Ascension Day/Sunday or All Saints' Day/Sunday. The third option includes the paraphrase of Revelation 7:12 by Horatius Bonar and is sung to the tune O QUANTA QUALIA. *The fourth variant is my own musical setting of the same text. The keyboard accompaniment appears on page 207.*

Leader: Salvation belongs to our God who sits upon the throne
           and to the lamb!   —Revelation 7:10

All: **Amen.**

or

Leader: Salvation belongs to our God who sits upon the throne
               and to the lamb!   —Revelation 7:10

All: **Amen.**
               Blessing and glory and wisdom
               and thanksgiving and honor and power and might
               be to our God forever and ever! Amen.   —Revelation 7:12

or

Leader: Salvation belongs to our God who sits upon the throne
               and to the lamb!   —Revelation 7:10

All: **Amen!**

All: *Singing*   O QUANTA QUALIA
               Blessing and honor and glory and power,
               Wisdom and riches and strength evermore
               Give we to Christ who our battle has won,
               Whose are the kingdom, the crown, and the throne.

                                              Words: Horatius Bonar, 1866, alt.

            or

Leader: Salvation belongs to our God who sits upon the throne
               and to the lamb.   —Revelation 7:10

All: **Amen.**

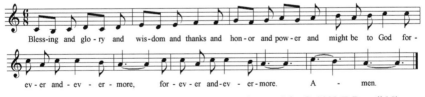

            Words: Revelation 7:12; music copyright © 2001 F. Russell Mitman.

◆◆◆   3.4.13

Another praise response for Trinity Sunday or general use is the following, which tradition
has wedded to the tune NICAEA.

Holy, Holy, Holy! Lord God Almighty!
All your works shall praise your name in earth and sky and sea;
Holy, Holy, Holy! merciful and mighty!
God in three Persons, blessed trinity!   Words: Reginald Heber, 1826, alt.

◆◆◆ 3.4.14

The following text is generally sung to the tune, LASST UNS ERFREUEN. *Without the alleluias it also may be sung to any of several long meter tunes such as* OLD HUNDREDTH, PUER NOBIS NASCITUR, *or the* TALLIS CANON, *which also may be sung as a round.*

From all that dwell below the skies let the Creator's praise arise;
Alleluia! Alleluia!
Let the Redeemer's name be sung through ev'ry land, in ev'ry tongue.
Alleluia, alleluia, alleluia, alleluia, alleluia!   Words: Isaac Watts, 1719, alt.

◆◆◆ 3.4.15

Charles Wesley wrote the following words in 1739 as the first stanza of an eighteen-stanza hymn to commemorate his conversion. Generally most hymnals begin the hymn with stanza seven, "O for a thousand tongues to sing. . . ." The text is frequently set to the tune AZMON, *although* RICHMOND *is an alternative.*

Glory to God, and praise and love be ever, ever given,
by saints below and saints above, the church in earth and heaven.
                                         Words: Charles Wesley, 1739

◆◆◆ 3.4.16

The following is designed for the festival of Christ the King/Reign of Christ. The musical setting of the ancient canticle Gloria Patri *may be used generally as a praise response, particularly appended to the Psalms or as a response to Scripture readings. A keyboard accompaniment appears on page 208.*

Leader: Great and amazing are your deeds, O God, the Almighty!

All: **Just and true are your ways, O Sovereign of the nations!**

Leader: Lord, who will not revere you and glorify your name?

All: **For you alone are holy.**

Leader: All nations will come and worship before you,

All: **for your judgments have been revealed.**   —Revelation 15:3a–4, adapt.

All: *Singing or speaking*

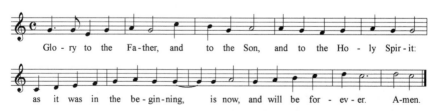

Glo - ry to the Fa - ther, and to the Son, and to the Ho - ly Spir - it:
as it was in the be - gin - ning, is now, and will be for - ev - er. A-men.

Words: *Consultation on Common Texts,* 1992;
Music copyright © 2004 F. Russell Mitman, 2004

◆◆◆ 3.4.17

The following penitential act is based on Isaiah 55:6–12 and includes a call to repentance, a prayer of confession, words of assurance, and a praise response. May it serve as a model for the structure of penitential acts.

Leader: Come, and seek the Lord who is to be found,
call upon the God who is near.

All: **Let the wicked forsake their way,
and the unrighteous their thoughts.**

Leader: Let us return to the Lord, that God may have mercy on us,

All: **And to our God, who will abundantly pardon.**

Unison: **O God, whose thoughts are not our thoughts,
and whose ways are not our ways;
we confess the rebel thoughts
that sever us from our dependence on you,
and we acknowledge the disobedient ways
that lead us from your paths of holiness and righteousness.
There is a vast difference between where we are
and where you intend us to be.
Yet, we ask for your unbounded love to find us in our sin,
to rescue us from ourselves,
to lead us to the living waters that restore,
and to give us the bread of life that fills us with good things;
through the grace of Jesus Christ. Amen.**

Leader: Hear the promises of God:
You shall go out in joy, and be led back in peace;
the mountains and the hills before you shall burst into song,
and all the trees of the field shall clap their hands.

All: **Thanks be to God!**

The Gloria in Excelsis, Gloria Patri, *or a doxology may be sung.*

Chapter Four

Word

It would hardly be wise to devote this section to suggested readings of Scripture and collections of sermons, for these would, in my estimation, contradict the meaning and purpose of the Word act itself. There are ample lectionaries, including the most widely used ecumenical *Revised Common Lectionary,* that provide direction in the weekly ordering of corporate worship. Also, I believe that once a sermon has been preached, it never really can be preached again. In published form sermons are either textbooks in the art of preaching or materials for devotions. They have passed the moment of fresh witness and must be relegated to history. One pastor remarked that the best thing that ever happened to him was that the movers lost his file of sermons when he was transferred from his last parish! All I dare attempt in this section is to comment on the nature of the Word act and to provide some resources to accompany it.

I choose the designation "Word act" specifically to point up the intrinsic unity of the reading and preaching of the Word. Both are one act in all historic and contemporary liturgies, because together each aims at witnessing to and conveying the one eternal Word made flesh and dwelling among us full of grace and truth. That Word is not something we can manipulate in a sermon. Rather, the words of the sermon only intend to be vehicles by which — upon the basis of the witness of Scripture — we may be questioned by that one Word made flesh in Jesus Christ. Hence, as indicated in the introduction, I suggest that pastors utilize a lectionary or the *lectio continuo* approach to ensure that preaching is not directed by the preacher's personal whim but by the confronting otherness of the Word of God. This means that the reading of Scripture and the preaching of the sermon are in principle and practice one unified act that should not be divided by extraneous material.

I choose the above terminology also because the Word act is unified with another act, namely, the Eucharist, wherein the Word is actualized and realized by Christ's presence with us in time to nourish us continually until the end of time. For Luther, there was only one sacrament, Jesus

Christ, with whom we are signed by God through baptism, preaching, and the Eucharist. To Calvin also, the Word read and preached was a sign through which Christ approaches people and effects his reign. From this perspective, just as a sermon without Scripture is merely a moral lecture, so too a service of Holy Communion without Scripture and sermon is only half a service. The realization that God comes to us in both Word and Sacrament was the overwhelming discovery of the Reformation in the sixteenth century and of the Second Vatican Council in the twentieth.

Essentially, the unified act of reading and preaching the Word is an oral and aural one. The words of Scripture are intended to be read aloud and listened to. Without trying to minimize the importance of Bible study as a preparation for worship, I believe that in the liturgy of worship the emphasis ought to be more on the corporate act of speaking and hearing the Word than on the private reading and studying of the words of the texts. The reading and preaching purposes to be an act in which we are addressed by God beyond the text and the preacher's words. That seems to be an important corrective in a day of intensified biblical literalism. Exegetical backgrounds to the texts are better kept to the sermon itself rather than to preemerge as lengthy and scholarly introductions to the lessons. I personally find it offensive to be forced to listen to a preface to the reading of the texts that tells me what the texts are saying. I believe that the Word of God is spoken by God through the Holy Spirit as the words of Scripture are read aloud and through the preaching of the sermon. What God has to say cannot be encapsulated in some few introductory sentences. Moreover, the prayer for the illumination of the Holy Spirit is for Scripture *and* sermon. The frequently invoked "May the words of my mouth . . ." by the preacher at the beginning of the sermon, in my mind, is not only redundant but self-assuming. Hopefully God already has begun to make the Word plain in the reading of the Scriptures and will continue to speak throughout the sermon and long after the preacher's last word. Also, the lessons ought to be read from an authoritative translation of the Bible rather than from paraphrases. The insight given through paraphrases ought to be relegated to the sermon time. Finally, it appears liturgically more appropriate for the reading of Scripture, like the preaching of the sermon, to be aural and oral; that is, the whole congregation ought not to be preoccupied with their own private reading in pew Bibles or lectionary inserts in the bulletins; and those bereft of aural abilities (the deaf) ought to have the Scripture and sermon signed. Pew Bibles and lectionary inserts are better used as references to which people may be directed for clarification of the text during the sermon. All these approaches aim at underlining the theological understanding that the authority of the Word lies not in the words of the texts themselves but in the eternal Word of God.

If we see the Word act, then, primarily as God's speaking to us, even through the frail words of human language and understanding, it is appropriate and necessary for the Word act to begin in the posture of prayer. The historic Reformed liturgies handled it with a sense of awe and prefaced the reading of Scripture with a prayer for illumination either extempore (Calvin) or written (Bucer) that God might actualize the Word in our hearing it read and preached. The Lutheran and Anglican services, based on the liturgical calendar, preserved the same perspective through the corresponding weekly collect.

Likewise, the historic liturgies followed the lessons and sermon with prayers of intercession. Somehow, over the years, the so-called pastoral prayer developed as an entity unto itself and in many churches got pushed prior to the sermon, sometimes sandwiched between Scripture and sermon. However, if we are faithful to history and to the organic structure of the divine-human interaction, it appears that our prayers of intercession are rightfully a *response* to the Word. The Word moves us to pray for ourselves and for others. The prayers may be prefaced by a general prayer that asks that what was witnessed to in the reading and preaching may be realized in our lives or by a prayer that asks that we may approach our praying in honesty and with integrity. Luther and Calvin included paraphrases of the Lord's Prayer in their intercessory prayers seemingly as a warrant for prayer and as a teaching of what prayers should be. Both assumed that the service would continue with the Eucharist, and thus the prayers led naturally to what was to follow. The prayers of the church are the bridge that links the Word act with the Eucharist.

The question of written or extemporary prayer still haunts congregations today. Struggling against the remnants and ravages of revivalism, churches at the midpoint of the twentieth century thought extemporary prayers quite unsophisticated. Beautiful prayers well written by the minister or, preferably, read from anthologies of prayers — all with the proper Elizabethan forms of the second person singular and structured in the five-fold style of the English collect — were deemed worthy and proper for a world come of age. The resurgence of pentecostalism and the charismatic movement since then have turned the tables and indicted anything not prompted on the spot as evidence that the pray-er (and also the preacher!) had not yet received enough measure of the Spirit. Historically, however, worship has never been an either/or situation. The early church, fresh with the Spirit's Pentecost initiative, nevertheless preserved the written and memorized prayers of its Hebrew past. Calvin's liturgies included both written prayers that were used each week and opportunities for extemporary prayer. The perspective that seems most appropriate in an age of alternatives is one of both/and.

Another element central to the Word act is the affirmation of the efficacy of the Word. We need to say that we believe the promise of the Gospel is for us. If baptism and its related acts are to be celebrated, here seems the appropriate place. If not, then that which developed from the ancient baptismal formula, namely, the Apostles' Creed, may serve as the symbol of faith. Other creeds or statements of faith, Scripture passages such as Philippians 2:6–11, or even congregational covenants are also appropriate expressions of this affirmation. In most contemporary liturgies the creed or statement of faith occurs between sermon and prayers. Calvin, however, placed the creed after the intercessions as a kind of transition between Word and Eucharist and as a sign of the commitment necessary for sharing in the Holy Communion. It was during the creed that the elements were prepared in Geneva, and, since there was no offertory in Calvin's service, the creed served as a bridge between Word and Eucharist. Today it appears that there may be occasions when creedal formulae may appropriately follow the sermon or homily, and there may be times also when, as in Calvin's liturgy, they may follow the prayers, especially if there is no offering to be received. In either case, the affirmation is integral to the Word act. In some liturgies still in use, the creed appears as a response to the lessons. This placement, however, seems to bifurcate the reading and preaching into two separate acts. Most of the recent liturgies — Lutheran, Reformed, Anglican, Methodist, and Roman Catholic — have restored the creed as a response to both reading and preaching.

The Word act may conclude with the ancient exchange of the peace whether or not the Eucharist is celebrated. The traditional wordings are variants of "Peace be with you," and verbally, at least, the phrase has survived as a ministerial act in some communion liturgies. There have been attempts in the last decades to make it a congregational act as well with the physical aspects of a hand clasp or embrace. I can remember elaborate directions being given to instruct the congregation how to exchange the peace correctly. I have the feeling that some people's initial reservations resulted from this stilted approach; it forced them to do something that had been unheard of in an Anglo-Saxon environment where people don't touch each other. For it to be an appropriate and meaningful gesture of Christian love and community, we need to allow the exchange of peace to be a natural expression rather than some arcane rite that needs rubrics and commentaries to be understood and appreciated. A simple and unstructured greeting without being concerned about the proper wording and motions is sufficient. The interaction itself ought to create the words and gestures.

Another alternative act that may occur here is the act of laying on hands for healing. Although most healing rites are designed as separate services, it is also appropriate for them to occur during regular weekly services of Word and Sacrament. Occasional opportunities may be given at the end of the intercessory prayers for the church to fulfill its commission of extending Christ's healing ministry. This enables the congregation to understand that the act of healing is part of its ongoing ministry of caring for people, and it may assure those who desire to receive the laying on of hands that this gesture is not the occult ritual sensationalized by TV faith healers.

There is the ever-present danger that the Word act might become a clerical prerogative. Chancel rails, rood screens, inaccessible pulpits, and other architectural barriers continue to foster the idea that the Word is something to be handled only by the clean hands of the clergy. But the days are over when the *clericus* is the only literate person and therefore the only one who can read and preach and pray. I feel it should be normative for the laity — a label I don't like — to participate fully in the Word act by regularly reading the lessons, sharing on occasions in preaching and regularly bringing the petitions and intercessions of the people before God. In some churches — particularly those of Hispanic traditions — most of the service is led by lay leaders, and only the sermon is the prerogative of the pastor. Requests for prayers may be made earlier in the service or before worship and brought to the altar table where prayers are offered by clergy and laity. Or, with care, the opportunity may be given for prayers, either extemporary or written, to be offered by members of the congregation at their seats. And by all means, some of the prayers ought to be prayed in unison.

I believe that lecterns are superfluous pieces of furniture designed more for aesthetic than for liturgical reasons. I think it more appropriate for readers to stand in place in the congregation or to enter the pulpit for the praying of the prayer of illumination and the reading of the lessons. It may be interesting also, as in the ancient liturgy of Hippolytus, for the reader to carry the Bible into the midst of the people where it is read. Pulpits are not the private domain of the clergy, and we need to make them physically much more accessible so that they can be literally the "platforms" for all the ministers — clergy and laity alike — in the reading and proclaiming of the Word. The same can be said of our altar tables, but we will reserve comment on that for later.

Another tool to help counteract clericalism and to relate Scripture to preaching is the creation of a group of people who regularly study the texts with the one preaching prior to the Sunday service and provide feedback following it. The concept of using such groups is not a novelty. The English Puritans and the Continental Reformed groups held weekly preaching workshops that they called "prophesying." This shared approach assumes that the needs and concerns of the congregation will be raised and addressed in the sermon. It also forces the preacher to do the exegetical work prior to Saturday evening!

PRAYERS FOR ILLUMINATION _____

◆◆◆   4.1.1

Holy God, who inspired your faithful people of old
to proclaim the promise of your coming,
by your Holy Spirit awaken us to your Word,
that, casting off the ways of darkness and night,
we may walk in the light of a new day of promise and hope;
through Jesus Christ our Lord. Amen.

◆◆◆   4.1.2

O God, who has caused all holy Scriptures to be written,
by your Holy Spirit illumine us as we read and hear them,
that through the encouragement they give us,
we may maintain our hope with fortitude,
and with one mind and one voice
praise the God and Father of our Lord Jesus Christ. Amen.

◆◆◆   4.1.3

O Word made flesh, dwelling among us full of grace and truth,
enlighten us with your true light, that we may behold your glory and receive,
from the fulness of your grace, the power to be born anew as children of God. Amen.

◆◆◆   4.1.4

The following is to be sung in unison to the tune BREAD OF LIFE.

**Break now the bread of life, dear Lord, to me,
as once you broke the loaves beside the sea.
Beyond the sacred page I seek you, Lord;
my spirit waits for you, O living Word!**

Words: Mary A. Lathbury, 1877, alt.

◆◆◆   4.1.5

Reader: Open our eyes, O God:

All: **That we may behold wondrous things out of your law.**

Reader: Open our ears, O God:

All: **That we may hear what you will speak to those
who turn to you in their hearts.**

Reader: Open our minds, O God:

All: **That we may understand what it means to revere you
and to learn of your ways.**

Reader: Open our hearts, O God:

All: **That we may grasp the treasures of wisdom and knowledge
hidden in Christ.**

Reader: Open our mouths, O God:

All: **That we may proclaim the mystery of the Gospel
and speak of it boldly.**

◆◆◆   4.1.6

O God, who prompted holy apostles
to proclaim the good news of Jesus' resurrection victory,
grant that as we listen to their witness,
the convincing power of your Holy Spirit
will confirm our faith that Jesus is the Christ,
and that through this faith we may receive new life in his name. Amen.

◆◆◆   4.1.7

*The following is designed to be sung, by the congregation as a whole, by a choir, or by a
soloist, who also may be the one designated to read the Scripture lesson(s). The suggested tune
is* MENDON.

Come, gracious Spirit, heav'nly Dove,
with light and comfort from above;
The light of truth to us display,
and make us know and choose your way.

Words: Simon Browne (1680–1732), alt.

◆◆◆ 4.1.8

O God, who by your Holy Spirit
moved your faithful servants of old to speak your word,
and by your impulse caused the Scriptures to be written,
interpret them to us in this reading,
that they may be fulfilled in our hearing today,
through Jesus Christ. Amen.

◆◆◆ 4.1.9

The following is designed to be sung as a corporate prayer. The tune traditionally associated with these words is HERR JESU CHRIST, *although there are other tunes equally suitable:* O WALY WALY, DUKE STREET, QUEBEC, *and* ROCKINGHAM.

Lord Jesus Christ, be with us now,
and let your Holy Spirit bow
all hearts in love and awe today,
to hear the truth and keep your way.

After the reading of the Scripture(s), the following stanza may be added as a response.

Glory to God, the Father, Son,
and Holy Spirit, Three in One!
To you, O blessed Trinity,
be praise throughout eternity!

Words: Wilhelm II, Duke of Saxe-Weimar, 1638, trans. Catherine Winkworth, 1862, alt.

◆◆◆ 4.1.10

Grant us an understanding mind, O God,
that in our reading and hearing this day
we may approach and be grasped by your eternal word.
By your Holy Spirit
inspire us with the wisdom that comes from on high,
and assist us to respond in lives of faithful obedience;
through Jesus Christ our Lord. Amen.

◆◆◆   4.1.11

The following is designed to be sung in unison to the tune FOREST GREEN.

Shine forth, O Light, that we may see with hearts all unafraid
the meaning and the mystery of things that you have made.
O Light of light! within us dwell, through us your radiance pour,
that word and life your truth may tell, and praise you evermore.

Words: Washington Gladden, 1897, alt.

◆◆◆   4.1.12

Grant us, O God, your Holy Spirit to reveal
the things beyond our seeing and hearing and imagining
which you have prepared for those who love you,
that we may share in the depths of your wisdom,
understand the spiritual gifts you have bestowed on us,
and speak of them in words found not by our human wisdom,
but alone through the gift of your Spirit. Amen.

—adapted from 1 Corinthians 2:9–13

◆◆◆   4.1.13

It was customary in Germany for part of a hymn to be sung before the sermon and the remaining stanzas to be sung after it. The following is adapted from one such Predigtlied, *or sermon hymn. However, it appears best to sing it before the reading of the lessons. The tune is the first four lines of* LIEBSTER JESU. *Since lines 1 and 2 are the same melody as lines 3 and 4, it may be sung antiphonally, as indicated, by two groups within the congregation, by choir and congregation, or by a soloist/reader and the congregation.*

Group 1: Gracious Giver of the Word,
               we are gathered all to hear you.

Group 2: Let our hearts and souls be stirred
               now to wait in awe before you.

Group 1: All our knowledge, sense, and sight
               lie in deepest darkness shrouded,

Group 2: till your Spirit breaks our night
               with the beams of truth unclouded.

Group 1: Glorious God, to us impart
               light from highest heav'n proceeding.

Group 2: Open now our ears and heart,
               as we hear this holy reading.

Words: Tobias Clausnitzer, 1663, trans. Catherine Winkworth, 1858, alt.

◆◆◆   4.1.14

The following may be prayed by the reader or responsively by reader and congregation.

We listen for your voice, O Lord God;
　　prepare us to hear it.
We expect your word;
　　help us to accept it.
We await your wisdom;
　　teach us to understand it.
We seek your truth;
　　show us how to find it.
We ask for your guidance;
　　strengthen us to follow it.
We want to know your will;
　　free us to do it.

SCRIPTURE VERSICLES _____

◆◆◆   4.2.1

In the following the responses before and after the Gospel reading may be said or sung. The accompaniment may be found on page 208.

Reader:　The _____ lesson for the _____ Sunday _____ is recorded in the
　　　　　_____ .

The Scripture lesson is read.

Reader:　The word of the Lord.

All:　**Thanks be to God.**

Reader:　The good news of Christ is recorded in the Gospel according to _____,
　　　　　the _____ chapter, beginning to read at the _____ verse.

Glo - ry be to you, O Lord.

The Gospel lesson is read.

Reader:　This is the Gospel.

Praise   be   to   you,   O   Christ.

◆◆◆   4.2.2

Reader: Listen for the word of God in a reading from _____ .

The lesson is read.

Reader: Bless to us, O God, this reading and hearing of your holy word.

All: **To your name be glory and praise. Amen.**

◆◆◆   4.2.3

Reader: Let anyone who has an ear
           listen to what the Spirit is saying to the churches.   —Revelation 2:7

◆◆◆   4.2.4

Reader: The _____ lesson is recorded in _____ . Listen for the Word of God.

◆◆◆   4.2.5

Reader: Here ends the lesson.

All: *Singing or speaking*
           Let your word abide in us, O Lord.

◆◆◆   4.2.6

Reader: Here ends this reading of the holy Scriptures.

All: **Blessed are those who hear and who keep what is written in it.**
                                                            —Revelation 1:3

◆◆◆   4.2.7

Reader: The grass withers, the flower fades,

All: **but the word of our God will stand forever.**   —Isaiah 40:8

◆◆◆ 4.2.8

Reader: Sanctify us in the truth, O God.

All: **Your Word is truth** —John 17:17, adapt.

◆◆◆ 4.2.9

This may follow an Old Testament or Epistle Lesson:

Reader: Thanks be to you, O God, for giving us your holy word.

◆◆◆ 4.2.10

The following responses may come after a Gospel lesson. The tunes for the hymn-responses are indicated accordingly.

Reader: Praise be to you, O Christ, for this your holy Gospel.

or

Reader: This is the good news!

All: **Praise to you, Lord Jesus Christ!**

All: *Singing* SICILIAN MARINERS
Thanks we give and adoration for your Gospel's joyful sound;
May the fruits of your salvation in our hearts and lives abound.
Ever faithful, ever faithful, to the truth may we be found.
Words: John Fawcett, 1773, alt.

or

Reader: This is the good news of Jesus Christ!

All: *Singing* CHRISTUS DER IST MEIN LEBEN
Abide with us, our Savior, sustain us by your Word,
That we may, now and ever, find peace in you, O Lord. Amen.
Words: Joshua Stegmann, 1632, alt.

PREFACES TO THE SERMON _____

◆◆◆ 4.3.1

Grace to you and peace, from God our Father, and the Lord Jesus Christ.

—Romans 1:7b

◆◆◆ 4.3.2

Peace to all of you who are in Christ.   —1 Peter 5:14

◆◆◆ 4.3.3

To those who are called, who are beloved in God
may mercy, peace, and love be yours in abundance.   —Jude 1:1b–2, adapt.

◆◆◆ 4.3.4

Grace to you and peace
from the One who is and who was and who is to come.   —Revelation 1:4, adapt.

ASCRIPTIONS OF PRAISE
TO FOLLOW THE SERMON _____

◆◆◆ 4.4.1

Blessed be the God and Father of our Lord Jesus Christ,
who has blessed us in Christ with every spiritual blessing.   —Ephesians 1:3

◆◆◆ 4.4.2

Leader: Now to the One who by the power at work within us
          is able to accomplish abundantly far more
          than all we can ask or imagine,

All: **to God be glory in the church
          and in Christ Jesus to all generations,
          forever and ever. Amen.**   —Ephesians 3:20–21, adapt.

◆◆◆ 4.4.3

Leader: To Christ who loves us and freed us from our sins by his blood,

All: **To him be glory and dominion forever and ever. Amen.**

—Revelation 1:5b, 6, adapt.

◆◆◆ 4.4.4

Leader: Blessed be the God and Father of our Lord Jesus Christ!

All: **By God's great mercy
we have been given a new birth into a living hope
through the resurrection of Jesus Christ from the dead.**

—1 Peter 1:3–4, adapt.

◆◆◆ 4.4.5

May grace and peace be yours in abundance
in the knowledge of God and of Jesus our Lord.   —2 Peter 1:2

◆◆◆ 4.4.6

Leader: Blessing and glory and wisdom and thanksgiving
and honor and power and might
be to our God forever and ever!

All: **Amen and amen!**   —Revelation 7:12, adapt.

◆◆◆ 4.4.7

Leader: Now to the One who is able to keep you from falling,
and to make you stand without blemish
in the presence of glory with rejoicing,

All: **To the only God our Savior, through Jesus Christ our Lord,
be glory, majesty, power, and authority,
before all time and now and forever. Amen.**   —Jude 1:24–25, adapt.

AFFIRMATIONS _____

◆◆◆ 4.5.1

*In the following, the Apostles' Creed, which had its origin in baptismal practices, is
shaped in the question-and-answer form of some ancient liturgies. The text of the Creed
is the ecumenical version prepared by the English Language Liturgical Consultation
(ELLC), 1988.*

Leader: In Christ, you have heard the word of truth, the Gospel of your salvation.

All: **We believe in Christ and are marked with the seal
of the promised Holy Spirit.**   —Ephesians 1:13–14

Leader: Living together in trust and hope,

All: We confess the faith of our baptism.

The congregation may stand.

Leader: Do you believe in God?

All: **I believe in God, the Father almighty,
            Creator of heaven and earth.**

Leader: Do you believe in Jesus Christ?

All: **I believe in Jesus Christ, God's only Son, our Lord,
            who was conceived by the Holy Spirit,
            born of the Virgin Mary,
            suffered under Pontius Pilate,
            was crucified, died, and was buried;
            he descended to the dead.
            On the third day he rose again;
            he ascended into heaven,
            he is seated at the right hand of the Father,
            and he will come to judge the living and the dead.**

Leader: Do you believe in the Holy Spirit?

All: **I believe in the Holy Spirit,
            the holy catholic church,
            the communion of saints,
            the forgiveness of sins,
            the resurrection of the body,
            and the life everlasting. Amen.**

◆◆◆ 4.5.2

Leader: Let the same mind be in you that was in Christ Jesus:

All: **Christ, though he was in the form of God,
            did not regard equality with God
            as something to be exploited,
            but emptied himself,
            taking the form of a slave,
            being born in human likeness.
            And being found in human form,
            he humbled himself
            and became obedient to the point of death—
            even death on a cross.**

Leader: Therefore God also highly exalted him
              and gave him the name that is above every name,

All: So that at the name of Jesus every knee should bend,
               in heaven and on earth and under the earth,
               and every tongue should confess
               that Jesus Christ is Lord, to the glory of God. — Philippians 2:5–11, alt.

PRAYER VERSICLES _____

◆◆◆   4.6.1

Rejoice in the Lord always; Rejoice, the Lord is near!
Do not worry about anything,
but in everything by prayer and supplication with thanksgiving,
let us make our requests known to God.   —Philippians 4:4–6, adapt.

◆◆◆   4.6.2

Leader: The Lord be with you.

All: **And also with you.**

Leader: Let us pray.

◆◆◆   4.6.3

Leader: As a deer longs for flowing streams,

All: **so my soul longs for you, O God.**
               My soul thirsts for God, for the living God.   —Psalm 42:1–2a

◆◆◆   4.6.4

Leader: Lift up your hearts!

All: **We lift them to God!**

Leader: Let us pray.

PRAYERS OF PETITION AND INTERCESSION _____

◆◆◆ 4.7.1

Although the following is designed so that the bids may be spoken by one person and the petitions by another, both bids and petitions may be prayed by one person, allowing periods for silent prayer between the bids and the petitions.

1. In peace, and for the peace that passes all understanding, let us pray to God.

2. Holy One, whose promise to the prophets was the gift of one to be called the Prince of Peace, we come before you as ones standing between promise and fulfillment. The light of peace has shined into our darkness through the gift of your Son, Jesus Christ. Yet the fulfillment of that peace lies beyond our immediate grasp. Grant us the vision of faith to follow the promise to Bethlehem's stall and to allow one more gift of Bethlehem's Gift to come to birth in our mangers. When our vision is dimmed by the glitter that catches our eyes, and our ears are deafened by immediate sounds that bombard us, grant us visions of things unseen, and speak to us sounds of words yet unheard, that in joy we may be surprised by Bethlehem's Child and the promised peace.

1. Rejoicing in everything, by prayer and supplication with thanksgiving, let us make our requests known to God.

2. Break through our anxieties, O Compassionate One, with the assurance that you are close at hand, keeping our hearts and minds in Christ Jesus.

   For those who dwell in the darkness of despair, hear our humble supplications.

   For those who suffer pain that pierces deeply, hear our humble supplications.

   For those who are sick, and especially for _____ , hear our humble supplications.

   For those who mourn, and especially for _____ , hear our humble supplications.

   For those who ask special requests unknown to us, yet alone known to you, hear our humble supplications.

   For those who have found peace in healing, for those lifted up by your hand and comforted by your voice, and especially for _____ , receive our joyous thanksgiving.

1. In the peace of silence, let us make our individual requests known to God.

Silence

◆◆◆ 4.7.2

The following is designed for the bids to be sung a cappella by a cantor; however, they may be spoken as well. Periods of silence may occur between bids and petitions. The final "Rejoice" may be sung by a choir with or without accompaniment. There is no need for an additional prayer response.

1. O come, O come, Emmanuel, and ransom captive Israel that mourns in lowly exile here until the Son of God appear.

2. Come, O God, and redeem your world for whom you have given your only Son.

   Come to our world with a new day, with a new way, with a new hope, with a new promise of justice and righteousness, and with a new life amid our tired ways. We seem captive to ourselves, strangers in exile, and we have forgotten where our destiny lies.

1. O come, O Dayspring, come and cheer our spirits by your advent here; disperse the gloomy clouds of night, and death's dark shadow put to flight.

2. Come, O God, amid the precariousness of life, when fear rolls over us and uncertainty clouds our perceptions.

   Come and cheer our joyless lives with a fresh sense of your joy-filling presence.

   Come, and be with those whose lives are shadowed with illness and pain.

   Come with healing on your wings, and rest your hands upon _____ and upon all who suffer today.

   Come with a comforting awareness amid death's shadows, and rest your peace upon _____ and upon all who feel a deep absence.

1. O come, thou Wisdom from on high, and order all things far and nigh; to us the path of knowledge show, and cause us in your ways to go.

2. Come, O God, and guide us with wisdom that defies our human rationales. Teach us how dependent we are — dependent on each other and dependent so much more on your loving grace. Show us again Christ's way, and give us the courage to follow in obedience and in faith, believing where we cannot see, and hoping even against hope.

1. O come, desire of nations, bind all people in one heart and mind; bid envy, strife, and quarrels cease; fill the whole world with heaven's peace.

2. Come, O God, amid the cries of angry mobs and protesting masses.

   Come when frustration flares into violence and when one raises sword against another.

   Come, and settle our human quarreling with a touch of holy and heavenly peace.

   Come to nations and to those who lead nations with a new vision of peace.

   Come with a new desire when old remembrances push us to bloodshed and to the brink of annihilation.

1. Rejoice, rejoice, Emmanuel shall come to thee, O Israel.

◆◆◆ 4.7.3

The four following selections may be prayed by one or more persons. The hymn portion may be sung to FOREST GREEN *or* ST LOUIS.

1. O God, who broke the stillness of an adult night with the birth-cry of a child, break into our night with the good news of Bethlehem's child. Surprise our weariness with a new manger, that, amid the coldness of an impersonal world, we may behold again the miracle of time wrapped in diapers, and, with the eyes of faith, see and follow the infant Word made flesh dwelling among us, full of grace and truth.

2. O God of all children, we pray for your children throughout the whole wide earth this night. To those who are hungry give a piece of Bethlehem's bread; to those suffering from sickness and disease, give your spirit's healing touch; to those who are lonely give your assuring presence; to those who are abandoned, neglected, and abused give your motherly care; to those who feel estranged and angry give a sign they are loved; and to every mother's child of every race and every tongue give the precious gift of your grace, fulfilling every need with heavenly peace.

3. O God who came as the peace-bringing Christ, come again this night to a world that seems to have forgotten the ways of peace. Show us the foolishness of angry shouts, the futility of terrorism, and the emptiness of warlike threats. Teach us that in Jesus our Brother we all are but one family thrown together into a small world, totally dependent on each other and on your transcending care.

4. O God of Christmas, who came in quiet ways to simple people in unspectacular surroundings, come amid the silence of this holy place on this holy eve, and hear the prayers of ordinary people like us.

Silence

Unison: *Singing*
How silently, how silently, the wondrous gift is given!
So God imparts to human hearts the blessed peace of heaven.
No ear may hear his coming, but in this world of sin,
Where meek souls will receive him, still the dear Christ enters in.

Words: Phillips Brooks, 1868, alt.

◆◆◆ 4.7.4

1. In peace, and for the peace of the whole world, let us pray to the God of peace who sent Jesus, to be for us the Prince of Peace.

2. O God, we pray for the peace of Bethlehem's hillsides to come and rest upon our weary world this Christmastide. We find ourselves frustrated by world events that lie beyond our control. We are afraid of changing orders and unpredictable alliances. We are captive to the present and therefore unable to see beyond the

bad news that seems to greet us with each new day. Come, O God, promiser of peace and goodwill, come and rest with your peace on our angry world. Dispel our fear with the assurance of your governing hand, cast out our anger with the unchanging promise of peace, and release us from captivity to violent shouts and chanting mobs, that your peace may become incarnate in our world.

1. In love, and for the love incarnate in Bethlehem's Child, let us pray to the God of love:

2. You surprised a world, O God, by coming not in clashing thunder or flashing lights, but in the quiet and simple splendor of a child's radiant face. Invite us into this mystery of love beyond all loves, that we may be led to a new kind of love: a love that loves not by what we can get, but in what we can give, a love that counts not who is worthy to receive, but, beyond our human calculations, is showered freely on all. Show us the way of Bethlehem's Child, that seeing, we may believe, and believing, we may learn again how to love.

1. In hope, and for the fulfillment of our hopes and needs, let us pray to the God of hope:

2. In Bethlehem, in the place of bread, you fulfilled, O God, the needs of a hungering world. Satisfy again the needs of your people hungering and thirsting for wholeness. With the touch of your healing hand be with all who suffer; and especially hear our prayers for _____ . With the promising Shalom of resurrection, be with all who mourn today, and especially _____ . With the mysterious gift of your abiding presence, be with all your people, that our human hopes and dreams may find fulfillment in the hope of all ages, even Jesus Christ our Lord.

1. In silence, and for the answering presence of holy quietness, let us pray to the God who promises to hear our prayers.

Silence

◆◆◆ 4.7.5

1. In intercession for our world, let us pray to the Sovereign of the nations.

2. God of judgment and pardon, we pray for a world divided by pride and wounded in the battle of warring ideologies. We ask for healing in our national life; we ask for attempts at harmony among those in whose hands lies the public trust; we ask for peace among the nations and for the promise of goodwill among all people, that the fear that parades as pride and the anger that propagandizes as power may be cast out by a perfect love that humbles the proud and tames the mighty.

1. In love, and for the love that over and around us lies, let us pray to the One who first loved us.

2. God of our fathers and God of our mothers, God of our children, and God of our brothers and sisters, we pray for the relationships of family and friendship in

which you have placed us and called us. Dispel the self-pity that cripples relationships. Replace unattainable expectations with earnest desires to fulfill needs and loves. By your spirit, bless new relationships, and especially the marriage/union of _____ and _____; heal those relationships that have been wounded, confirm those that have been restored; and hear our prayers for those dear to us, whom we now name in silence.

Silence

1. In compassion, and for the healing of the human family, let us pray to the God who promises wholeness.

2. For people who find themselves in all sorts and conditions today: for those known to us and for those unknown, for all persons in need of healing and Shalom, and especially for _____, hear our prayers.

1. In silence, and in the promise that our prayers will be heard, let us pray to the God who listens in secret.

Silence

◆◆◆ 4.7.6

The following set of petitions and intercessions is shaped by Romans 5:1–11, which is appointed in the Revised Common Lectionary *for several Sundays in the three-year cycle. The bids and prayers may also be prayed by the same person. Periods of silence may be inserted between the bids and prayers.*

1. In hope born amid suffering, nourished in endurance, and tested in character, let us pray to the God of hope.

2. Thanks be to you, loving God, for your love poured into our hearts through your Holy Spirit:

>   love that gives us reason to hope amid the clouds we so much dread,
>   love that reaches beyond our finite imaginations,
>   love that breaks through all barriers with a hope that will not disappoint us.

In your mercy give us a steady courage to trust amid present sufferings that your promises will be fulfilled.

>   Save us from the easy roads that detour us from the race for endurance.
>   Save us, too, from the ways that demand no character.

But guide us by your Holy Spirit on the path that leads through crosses and Calvaries to a new hope dawning for the world in the resurrection of our Lord Jesus Christ.

1. In love poured into our hearts through the Holy Spirit, let us pray for the church of Jesus Christ.

2. We pray, O Christ of the church, for courage to be your responsible people. Save us from overlooking suffering and injustice, from being satisfied with the paths of least resistance, and from being caught up in trivia.

Renew our trust in your Gospel's alternative to the world's ways.
Strengthen our obedience to a way that seeks not to satisfy human wants but to fulfill human needs.

Shower us with the gracious gifts of the Holy Spirit, that we may be so bound together in love, that others may see in the church of Jesus Christ the only means of grace and the one promise of everlasting hope.

1. In the promise of hope that does not disappoint, let us pray for all people suffering today.

2. For those whose names are known and unknown to us,

for those whose names may even be our own names,

for all who suffer, hear our prayers, O God of healing and wholeness.

For those carrying the weight of pain, that they may know new meaning for that which they bear and may hope for healing by your grace.

For those who suffer the separation of death, that they may know, through patient endurance, the peace that now passes understanding.

And for all your people with needs known only to you, hear our prayers.

1. In the assurance that through faith in Christ Jesus we have obtained access to God's grace, let us pray for ourselves.

Silence

◆◆◆   4.7.7

God, whose love broke through death's dark prison in Jesus' resurrection, open wide your people to receive this transforming power, and hear now our Easter prayers.

In love outpoured from the cross on accusers and conspirators, betrayers and condemners, your Christ reconciled all his adversaries. So also, O God, we ask you to touch your world with his cleansing forgiveness, and give us the courage to reach out and forgive our enemies, that, rescued from the dark night of distrust and fear, your world may awaken to Easter's freedom to love and to trust. Empower your church in this and every place to proclaim boldly in word and deed the good news that, through the resurrection of Christ, love's redeeming work is done, and that men and women, youth and children everywhere may share, through word and sacrament, in the new life Christ gives.

Hear our prayers also for those chained to the past: those convicted by past sins and age-old guilt, those imprisoned by anxiety and loneliness, those captive to rigid ideas and worn-out attitudes. Give them the courage to release themselves from their dark tombs and to step out into the fresh new day filled with hope and confidence.

We pray, too, for those in special need of your resurrection love and saving grace today, that you will be with those whom we remember before you in silence.

Silence

Response: *Singing* PUER NOBIS NASCITUR
O Jesus, King of gentleness, with love and power our hearts possess, that we may give you all our days the willing tribute of our praise.

◆◆◆ 4.7.8

Leader: O God, Creator of all that was and is and shall be,

All: **Have mercy on us.**

Leader: O God, the Son, Redeemer of the world,

All: **Have mercy on us.**

Leader: O God, the Sanctifier of all of life,

All: **Have mercy on us.**

Leader: O holy, blessed, and glorious Trinity, one God ever with us,

All: **Have mercy on us.**

Leader: From failure to recognize your supporting hand
intervening in and guiding the affairs of people and nations,

All: **Holy God, deliver us.**

Leader: From insensitivity to the needs of people —
the hungry, the lonely, the prisoners, the sick, and the dying,

All: **Holy God, deliver us.**

Leader: From age-old divisions and newly devised rationales
that assail your church and fragment the body of Christ,

All: **Holy God, deliver us.**

Leader: That your people everywhere
may be filled with large visions and big dreams and new ideas
of what your world might be in that peace
which now passes our understanding,

All: **Enliven us, we pray.**

Leader:	That as Jesus came preaching, teaching, and healing, we who bear his name may be given the courage to tell the good news, to lead conscientiously in the way of truth, and to reach out in love,
All:	**Enliven us, we pray.**
Leader:	That the church, called by the Holy Spirit, may be strengthened in this place and united in every place throughout the whole wide earth,
All:	**Enliven us, we pray.**
Leader:	For supplying us with the good things that sustain us and for sharing with us the people who give meaning and hope to our lives,
All:	**We thank you, Creator.**
Leader:	For your saving love, born in a manger, laid bare on the cross, and resurrected beyond death,
All:	**We thank you, Christ.**
Leader:	For your renewing presence transforming the ordinary into mysteries beyond our minds' grasp,
All:	**We thank you, Holy Spirit.**
Unison:	**To you, One Holy and Undivided Trinity, be honor and glory, praise and thanksgiving, now and forevermore! Amen.**

or

Unison: *Singing*   NICAEA
                     Holy, holy, holy, God the Almighty!
                     All your works shall praise your name in earth and sky and sea.
                     Holy, holy, holy! Merciful and mighty!
                     God in three persons, blessed Trinity!

     4.7.9

The following is based on the hymn by John Greenleaf Whittier. The response may be said either by one person or by the congregation, or it may be sung by a soloist, by a choir, or by the entire congregation. A simple pedal note is sufficient to establish a pitch for singing. The tunes for singing are REST *or* REPTON.

Leader:	Let us pray for the world, and lift to God our intercessions for the world's order and societies, that the dark night of hatred and suspicion may pass away, and a new day of peace and goodwill may dawn.

Response: **Dear God, embracing humankind, forgive our foolish ways;**
        reclothe us in our rightful mind;
        in purer lives your service find,
        in deeper reverence, praise.

Leader: Let us remember before God this congregation
        and every church in every land,
        that we may respond to the Gospel command.

Response: **In simple trust like theirs who heard, beside the Syrian sea,**
        the gracious calling of the Lord,
        let us, like them, without a word
        rise up and followers be.

Leader: Let us intercede for all who need the special touch of God this day,
        remembering all who are sick and suffering, especially _____
        and all who mourn deeply the death of their loved ones,
        especially _____ , that they may find heaven's healing and peace.

Response: **Drop your still dews of quietness, till all our strivings cease;**
        take from our souls the strain and stress,
        and let our ordered lives confess
        the beauty of your peace.

Leader: Let us pray in silence for ourselves and bring to God our inmost thoughts.

Silence

Response: **Breathe through the heats of our desire your coolness and your balm;**
        let sense be dumb, let flesh retire;
        speak through the earthquake, wind, and fire,
        O still small voice of calm!

◆◆◆   4.7.10

1. Upon the promise made to Abraham and Sarah and to their posterity forever,
   let us pray to God, the Creator.

2. O God, whose love provides for the needs of your people,
   we commend to your love the world you have made.
   Save us from a smug self-sufficiency that assumes we can manipulate
   the order of nature and the affairs of people by our wanton control;
   but humble us to the awareness of our total dependence
   on your life-giving hand
   and of our intimate and precious relationship with every living thing,
   that your world may be in harmony.

1. Upon the promise made in Christ that the church shall be one,
   let us pray to God, the Reconciler.

2. O Christ who in love called us to be your body,
    we commend to your love your church throughout the whole wide earth.
    Keep us from aggravating the wounds suffered in the accidents of history,
    but turn us to the needs of a new and different world
    crying out for your reconciling love and justice,
    that with one mind and one heart,
    we may fulfill your mission of preaching, teaching, and healing.

1. Upon the promise of the risen Christ to grant us the Holy Spirit,
    let us pray to God, the Redeemer and Counselor.

2. O Holy Spirit, who empowers us to be a royal priesthood,
    we intercede for all those in need of your comforting presence:
    for the victims of natural and human disasters,
    for the aimless and the restless,
    for the sick and the dying, and especially for _____ ,
    that you will relieve them from distress
    and endow us with the spiritual gifts to minister to them in their needs.

All: Amen.

◆◆◆   4.7.11

The following is a structure for bidding prayers. The petitions may be altered and completed, depending on the circumstances.

1. Let us pray for the church.

2. O God, who with the Holy Spirit and through the laying on of hands
    founded and constituted the church of Jesus Christ,
    we pray for your church universal:

1. Let us pray for the world.

2. O God, who promised to our spiritual forebears
    the strength and fortitude to stand fast amid a cruel and hostile world,
    we pray for the world in which you have placed us today:

1. Let us pray for all in need.

2. O God, giver of the Holy Spirit, the Counselor and Comforter,
    we pray for all who need you in special ways today:

1. Let us pray for ourselves in silence.

Silence

◆◆◆   4.7.12

The following can serve also as a model for litany-type prayers. The petitions may be excluded, changed, or added to, depending on the circumstances. The responses may be said or sung to the tune below. If the responses are sung, a soloist or the choir may sing the "In your mercy,

O God" part in unison or in harmony, and the congregation may sing the "hear our prayer."
The keyboard accompaniment appears on page 209. It may also be downloaded from the CD.

Leader: Holy God, who assured us in Christ Jesus
         that whatever we ask in his name will be granted to us
         and who promised to intercede for us through the Holy Spirit,
         hear now the prayers of your people.

Leader: For the world you have fashioned
         and every living thing formed by your creating hand,
         that all your creatures may be in harmony,

Response: *Singing or speaking*

In your mer - cy, O God, hear our prayer.

Leader: For the peoples of earth,
         that they may acknowledge the common humanity that unites them
         and learn the ways of peace,

Response: *Singing or speaking*
         In your mercy, O God, hear our prayer.

Leader: For the leaders of all nations and states and communities,
         and especially for _____,
         that they may be led to govern wisely
         and to hasten the day when justice and righteousness shall fill all the earth,

Response: *Singing or speaking*
         In your mercy, O God, hear our prayer.

Leader: For one holy catholic church throughout the whole wide earth,
         and especially for _____ *(partner churches in foreign lands, missionaries,*
         denominational officials, ecclesiastical meetings, local church pastors and people
         may be mentioned),
         that the body of Christ may be built up in love,
         and faith nourished through Word and Sacrament,

Response: *Singing or speaking*
         In your mercy, O God, hear our prayer.

Leader: For the relationships uniting people in marriage and holy union,
         in family and friendship,
         and especially for _____ and _____,
         that they may be sustained by constant love
         and strengthened by ever-renewing commitment,

Response: *Singing or speaking*
In your mercy, O God, hear our prayer.

Leader: For those who find themselves victims of forces beyond their control:
for those oppressed in mind or body,
for those crushed by life's sudden changes,
for those enslaved by controlling ideologies or chemical addictions,
that they may be assured of your power to save and to free,

Response: *Singing or speaking*
In your mercy, O God, hear our prayer.

Leader: For those who suffer from the ravages of illness in body or mind,
for those who anxiously await diagnoses,
for those confined by infirmity, and especially for _____ ,
that they may be comforted by your abiding presence amid their pain
and find wholeness by your healing hand laid upon them,

Response: *Singing or speaking*
In your mercy, O God, hear our prayer.

Leader: For those who are dying,
for those to whom death has caused a great emptiness,
and especially for _____ ,
that they may be touched by a resurrecting peace
that now passes our understanding,

Response: *Singing or speaking*
In your mercy, O God, hear our prayer.

Leader: For all children born into the world,
and especially for the gift of a _____ to _____ ,
that they may be blessed as the ones to whom your kingdom belongs,

Response: *Singing or speaking*
In your mercy, O God, hear our prayer.

Leader: For ourselves and the things that,
deeply hidden within the recesses of our minds,
we now pour out before you in silence:

Silence

Response: *Singing or speaking*

In your mer - cy, O God, hear our prayer, and grant us your peace. A - men.

Music copyright © 1987 F. Russell Mitman

◆◆◆   4.7.13

The following may be prayed by more than one person in succession or alternatingly.

O God, who has made us your own people and called us into the household of faith and the body of Christ, we pray for your church in this place and in every place. When differing hopes and differing ideas threaten to separate us, give us a vision of a larger unity in Christ. Give us patience amid diversity, the will to bear together present burdens, and place ever before us the yearning of Christ, that the church may one day be one.

We pray, O God, for the world in which you have created us and placed us in kinship with people of every nation on earth. When others' ideologies threaten us and frustrate us, give us the patience to wait for your guidance in the course of human history. When violence provokes us to respond with violence, calm our fears with the awesome awareness of your loving forbearance. Give to all people who find themselves victims of forces beyond their control the patient yet steadfast hope of your sustaining presence and the assurance that your anointing oil shall never run dry.

We pray, too, for the little people of the world, those, who, in the constancy of faith, give their mites so that others may live. Grant them the saving assurance of your grace and the confirmation of their faith that salvation comes not by noteworthy deeds and newsworthy achievement, but alone by grace, and solely through faith.

Hear our prayers, also, O God of healing and health, for those who suffer from the ravages of disease and who await uncertain diagnoses. We pray for _____ , that you will lay your healing hand upon *him/her/them,* granting patience amid pain and uncertainty, and, if it be your will, the health and wholeness you have promised in Christ Jesus.

O God, who has united us in one communion with all the saints who have lived and died in Christ and with whom we are surrounded as a cloud of heavenly witnesses, we praise you for their lives of holy faith and for their kinship with us in the household of faith. We remember with thanks all those who have gone before us, and especially _____ , who *has/have* died in Christ. We continue to entrust *him/her/them* to your loving care and ask for your perpetual light to shine upon *him/her/them.* Grant to us, your church on earth, and to all who yet walk this way, the patience to follow in faith and to continue on our course in holiness, until we attain the blessed promise of heaven, our eternal home.

And now, O God, we pause to pray for ourselves, to cast upon you the burdens of our hearts and minds, in the promise that where two or three are gathered in the name of Jesus Christ, you will hear our prayers and grant our requests.

Silence

PRAYER RESPONSES ————————————————————

◆◆◆ 4.8.1

All: *Singing*   INTEGER VITAE
Father Almighty, bless us with your blessing,
Answer in love your children's supplications;
Hear now our prayers, the spoken and unspoken;
Hear us, Eternal God.

Words: L. J. W., in *The Sunny Side,* 1875, alt.

◆◆◆ 4.8.2

Leader: Hear our prayers, O Lord,

All: **and listen to our cries.**   —Psalm 39:12, adapt.

◆◆◆ 4.8.3

Leader: Hear our prayer, O God,

All: **And let our cries come to you.**

Leader: Hide not your face from us,

All: **And answer us when we call.**   —Psalm 102:1–2, adapt.

◆◆◆ 4.8.4

Various musical settings are available for the following ancient hymn by Richard of Chichester. The response also may be spoken in unison.

All: *Singing*
Day by day, dear Lord, of you three things I pray:
To see you more clearly, love you more dearly,
follow you more nearly, day by day.

◆◆◆ 4.8.5

The following may be sung to ST. LOUIS *or* FOREST GREEN.

All: *Singing*
O Holy Child of Bethlehem! Descend to us, we pray;
Cast out our sin and enter in; be born in us today.
We hear the Christmas angels the great glad tidings tell;
O come to us, abide with us, our Lord Emmanuel.

Words: Phillips Brooks, 1868

◆◆◆ 4.8.6

All: *Singing*   DIX
        Holy Jesus, every day keep us in the narrow way;
        And, when earthly things are past,
        bring our ransomed souls at last,
        where they need no star to guide,
        where no clouds your glory hide.

                            Words: William C. Dix, 1861, alt.

◆◆◆ 4.8.7

All: *Singing*   HEINLEIN
        Keep, O keep us, Savior dear, ever constant by your side,
        That with you we may appear at the eternal Eastertide.

                Words: George Hunt Smyttan, 1856, alt.

◆◆◆ 4.8.8

All: *Singing*   PUER NOBIS NASCITUR
        O Lord of all, with us abide in this our joyful Eastertide;
        From every weapon death can wield
        your own redeemed forever shield.

        Words: Latin, fifth century, trans. John M. Neale, 1851, alt.

◆◆◆ 4.8.9

Leader: Like fragrant incense set before you,

All: **Let our prayers come to you, O God.**   —Psalm 141:1–2, paraphrased.

◆◆◆ 4.8.10

All: *Singing*   ST. ANNE
        O God, our help in ages past,
        Our hope for years to come,
        Be now our guard while troubles last,
        And our eternal home.

                            Words: Isaac Watts, 1719

Chapter Five

Offertory

The history of the offertory could be a treatise unto itself. Perhaps no other part of the Sunday service has been so used, disused, or abused. We find it despised by the Reformers as smacking of the sacrifice of the mass. Since Calvin felt that the offering really takes place after the service, in the world where the Christian offers self to neighbor, Calvin abolished it from the Sunday service. Today it is often relegated to the status of a half-hearted collection of envelopes to pay the dues of membership in a voluntary church organization. Most of us look at it as a necessary evil and reserve it as time for choirs and organists to provide entertainment. Yet the offertory cries out for a recognition of its integrity and a revitalization of its expressions.

We can approach the offertory from either of two perspectives, yet arrive at the same definition. First, historically the offertory was part of the Eucharist. In the days of Gregory in the sixth century, there was movement and music throughout the offertory as the people — and the clergy! — brought their offerings of wine and loaves of bread and gifts for Christian charity to the altar table. Later — and this is what offended Luther, Calvin, and others — the offering was restricted to that of the priest in his sacrifice of the mass. Nevertheless, from the beginning, the offertory was intended as an act of congregational thanksgiving and as a preparation for the Eucharist.

Second, we reach the same meaning when we approach the offertory from the perspective of the divine-human interaction. When we are confronted by the Word of God, what is the natural response but an offering of ourselves in thanksgiving — with all the tangible symbols we have — and a physical and spiritual preparation to be fed and nourished with holy signs? We cannot affect a sacrifice. The sacrifice was made once and for all time on Golgotha. But we can offer praise and come with thanksgiving to be nourished as God, through the sacrament, enables us to partake of Christ's sacrifice for us.

Hence the emphasis at the offertory is not on things — in our day usually money — but on the act of offering ourselves (including our money and other gifts) that God may nourish us and commission us to lives of holiness. In this sense, the offertory is akin to presenting ourselves for baptism. If the focus is on the act of offering, then it seems appropriate for us to provide verbal and nonverbal ways to express the action. To help avoid the idea of a "collection," persons may be invited, if not limited by numbers and space, to make their offering at the altar table and to remain there for the Eucharist. If that is physically impossible, representatives of the congregation, including children, may bring forth the offerings and place them on or at the altar table along with the elements to be used in the Eucharist. Those appointed to serve the communion then may remain with the officiants for the remainder of the service. The offertory is a table-setting action. Thus, it is important that the elements not be present on the altar table until the offertory. The elements are part of the offering. Also, there's nothing wrong with money sitting on the altar table with the "holy" things. Money is literally the most powerful symbol of our being today, and its presence on the holy table may serve to remind us of the holiness and righteousness to which we are called through the use of our money. Incidentally, most of the vessels used in churches to receive people's tithes and offerings are remnants from the days when coins were what most people put in the plates. Symbolically those little plates communicate that God doesn't expect much stewardship return! In some ethnic churches large baskets are passed through the pews, and the message is that God gives abundantly and that God's people give generously.

But what about the Sundays when the Eucharist is not celebrated? As mentioned earlier, most contemporary and historic liturgies are so structured that the same service is used up to the offertory, whether or not the Eucharist is celebrated. If it is, the service continues following the offertory with the acts of the Eucharist. If the Eucharist is not celebrated, the service continues following the offertory with acts of thanksgiving and dismissal. In either case, the offertory foreshadows the Eucharist, and if it is not celebrated, the prayers of thanksgiving and commissioning replace the Eucharistic prayers. Therefore, as illustrated in the following resources, the prayers of thanksgiving are not just dedications of money. Rather, like the Eucharistic prayer before the communion, they recall God's saving deeds, and, like the post-communion thanksgiving, they commission us and propel us into the world in service. There is no need for a special prayer following the offering when the Eucharist is celebrated, and in a service without the Eucharist, there is no need either for dedication of money. In either case, the prayers are for the sanctification of all of life and for commissioning to service in the name of Christ. In reality, then, the offertory acts flow into acts of sending.

In most churches offertory acts are accompanied by some kind of music, and in my travels to different churches I have learned that there are a host of creative musical expressions that can be used to lift up the joy and thanks of the offertory. Whether these are offered by instrumentalists or choirs, the emphasis ought to be on the offering of God-given talent in praise and thanksgiving and not on the musicians' proficiency and performance. The offertory is not a time for a concert, nor for entertainment. It is also appropriate for the assembly to sing a hymn during the offertory, allowing the last verse to become the offertory response as the gifts are presented. A number of concertatos that involve choir and congregation have been composed for use at the offertory and also as a response. Often we get stuck in the rut of using the same offertory response week after week, year after year. I suggest changing the response seasonally, if not weekly, so that the offertory responses as all other worship acts are shaped by the Scriptures that inform each worship experience. In addition to some of the suggestions in this chapter, there are many other hymns and verses of hymns that can be used for a change of scenery. It's even possible to use a nonmusical choral reading as an offertory response. In conclusion, the offertory ought to reflect the whole variety of spiritual gifts with which God has endowed every congregation, large and small.

OFFERTORY RESPONSES _____

◆◆◆   5.1.1

WINCHESTER NEW

All praise to you, eternal Son, whose Advent has our freedom won.
Whom with the Father we adore, and Holy Spirit evermore.

Words: Charles Coffin, 1736; trans. John Chandler, 1837 alt.

◆◆◆   5.1.2

In most hymnals these stanzas of Georg Weissel's hymn "Open Wide the Door," translated as "Lift Up Your Heads, Ye Mighty Gates," are sung to the militaristic tune TRURO. *However, the words are given more gentle wings when set, as in Lutheran and German hymnals, to* HALLE, *in which both stanzas are sung as one. As two separate stanzas they also can be sung to* ROCKINGHAM *or* O WALY WALY.

Redeemer come! We open wide our hearts to you, here, Lord, abide!
With grace unbounded enter in, and deeds of love in us begin.

Your Holy Spirit lead us on until our glorious goal is won;
eternal praise, eternal fame be offered Savior, to your name!

Words: Georg Weissel, 1642, trans. Catherine Winkworth, 1862, alt.

◆◆◆   5.1.3

Then let us all with one accord   THE FIRST NOWELL
   sing praises to our heavenly Lord,
Who has made heav'n and earth of naught,
   and with his blood our life has bought.
Nowell, Nowell, Nowell, Nowell,
   born is the King of Israel.
or   born in a manger, Emmanuel.

◆◆◆   5.1.4

As with gladness those of old did the guiding star behold;   DIX
As with joy they hailed its light, leading onward, beaming bright;
So, most gracious God, may we evermore your glory see.

As they offered gifts most rare at the manger rude and bare,
So may we with holy joy, pure and free from sin's alloy,
All our costliest treasures bring, Christ to you, our heav'nly King!

Words: William C. Dix, 1861, alt.

◆◆◆   5.1.5

The following is an offertory hymn to be sung antiphonally by solo voice and congregation. It is designed to be used when the congregation gathers around the altar table for the celebration of Holy Communion. Worshipers place their monetary offerings in the plates on the altar table while singing.

Solo: What child is this, who, laid to rest,   GREENSLEEVES
        on Mary's lap is sleeping?
     Whom angels greet with anthems sweet,
        while shepherds watch are keeping?

All: **This, this is Christ the King**
     whom shepherds guard and angels sing;
     Haste, haste to bring him laud, the babe, the son of Mary.

Solo: Why lies he in such mean estate
        where ox and ass are feeding?
     Good Christian, fear for sinners here
        the silent Word is pleading.

All: **This, this is Christ the King**
                whom shepherds guard and angels sing;
                Haste, haste to bring him laud,
                the babe, the son of Mary.

Solo: So bring him incense, gold, and myrrh;
                  come, one and all, to own him;
                The King of kings salvation brings;
                  let loving hearts enthrone him.

All: **This, this is Christ the King**
                whom shepherds guard and angels sing;
                Haste, haste to bring him laud,
                the babe, the son of Mary.

Words: William C. Dix, 1865, alt.

◆◆◆ 5.1.6

O Jesus, we adore you, upon the cross, our King!   PASSION CHORALE
We bow our hearts before you, your gracious name we sing.
That name has brought salvation, that name in life our stay,
Our peace, our consolation when life shall fade away.

Arthur T. Russell, 1851, alt.

◆◆◆ 5.1.7

This response may be sung to any number of long meter tunes. Three suggestions are: PUER NOBIS NASCITUR, WINCHESTER NEW, *or* OLD HUNDREDTH. *The doxological verse "Praise God from whom all blessings flow" may be added to the singing of both stanzas or substituted for the second stanza. Note that "Praise God from whom all blessings flow,..." which traditionally is sung to* OLD HUNDREDTH, *is equally appropriate when set to the other tunes.*

O Jesus, King of gentleness, do all our inmost hearts possess
and we to you will ever raise the tribute of our grateful praise.

O Lord of all, with us abide in this our joyful Eastertide;
From every weapon death can wield your own redeemed forever shield.

Words: Latin hymn, fifth century, trans. John M. Neale, 1852, alt.

◆◆◆ 5.1.8

The following response may be sung in unison, or, as indicated, responsively by a choir or soloist and the assembly.

Choir/soloist: LASST UNS ERFREUEN
                All creatures, your creator bless,
                and worship God in humbleness,

All: O praise God, Alleluia!

Choir/soloist:
    Praise, praise the Father, praise the Son,
    and praise the Spirit, Three in One.

All: **Alleluia! Alleluia!, Alleluia! Alleluia! Alleluia!**
                        Words: Francis of Assisi, 1225, trans. William H. Draper, c. 1910, alt.

◆◆◆   5.1.9

We praise you, O God, our Redeemer, Creator,   KREMSER
In grateful devotion our tribute we bring.
We lay it before you, we kneel and adore you,
We bless your holy name, glad praises we bring.

With voices united our praises we offer,
To you, great Jehovah, glad anthems we raise;
Your strong arm will guide us, our God is beside us;
To you, our great Redeemer, forever be praise!
                                             Words: Julia C. Cory, 1902, alt.

◆◆◆   5.1.10

Wide as the world is God's command,   OLD HUNDREDTH
Vast as eternity God's love;
Firm as a rock God's truth must stand,
When rolling years shall cease to move.
                                             Words: Isaac Watts, 1719, alt.

The doxology "Praise God from Whom All Blessings Flow" may be added. Both stanzas also may be sung to WINCHESTER NEW.

◆◆◆   5.1.11

Folliott S. Pierpoint wrote the following hymn for the Eucharist. Although in most hymnals it has been abridged from its original eight stanzas and placed with opening or processional hymns, here it is adapted for use at the offertory — more in keeping with the author's intent.

The hymn is commonly set to a tune named after W. C. Dix, who first set it to the text "As with Gladness Men of Old," in 1861. Actually, the composer was Conrad Kocher, who had it published in a collection of German hymns twenty-three years earlier. Kocher's original had an interesting melodic treatment in the next to the last line. If this is used, as printed below, perhaps the first six verses should be sung no higher than in the key of G.

In this adaptation, the hymn is designed to be sung responsively while the offering is received. The stanzas may be sung by the choir and/or solo voices, and the refrain by the congregation. While this setting may be more interesting, the hymn also may be sung by the congregation in unison. At a moderate tempo (it is often sung much too fast in most

American churches) and with one verse by the organist as an introduction, about three minutes are afforded the ushers for receiving the people's offering. Following the versicle, the people stand, and, while the offering is presented, the organist may play all or a portion of the hymn to reestablish pitch. The final stanza, which also is the prayer of thanksgiving, should be sung in unison. No additional prayer is necessary. The service may continue with the Eucharist, and this liturgy may serve, as Pierpoint intended, as the Eucharistic prayer to which the offering is integral. If so used, the minister continues with the words of institution, and all pray the Lord's Prayer. After all have communed, the minister offers a prayer of thanksgiving. If the Eucharist is not celebrated, the service concludes with the Lord's Prayer and a dismissal act.

Minister: Let us thank God for steadfast love,

All: **for God's wonderful works to humankind.**

Minister: Let us offer a sacrifice of thanksgiving

All: **and tell of God's deeds with songs of joy.**   —Psalm 107:21–22, adapt.

Choir: For the beauty of the earth, for the beauty of the skies,   DIX
                 for the love which from our birth over and around us lies;

All:

Christ, our God, to you we raise this our sac - ri - fice of praise.

Choir: For the beauty of each hour of the day and of the night,
                 hill and vale, and tree and flower, sun and moon and stars of light:

All: **Christ our God, to you we raise, this our sacrifice of praise.**

Choir: For the joy of ear and eye, for the heart and mind's delight,
                 for the mystic harmony linking sense to sound and sight:

All: **Christ our God, to you we raise, this our sacrifice of praise.**

Choir: For the joy of human love, brother, sister, parent, child,
                 friends on earth, and friends above, for all gentle thoughts and mild:

All: **Christ our God, to you we raise, this our sacrifice of praise.**

Choir: For your church that evermore lifts up holy hands above,
                 offering up on every shore its pure sacrifice of love:

All: **Christ our God, to you we raise, this our sacrifice of praise.**

Choir: For the prophets' strong command, for your bold confessors' might,
                 for apostles' noble stand, for the martyrs' crown of light:

All: **Christ our God, to you we raise, this our sacrifice of praise.**

Minister: All giving is good, and every perfect gift comes from heaven above,

All: **From the God who brought us forth by the word of truth,**
            that we should become the first fruits of the new creation.
                                                    —James 1:17–19, adapt.

The offerings are brought to the altar table during the following stanza.

All: *Singing*
            For each perfect gift sublime unto us so freely given,
            Graces, human and divine, peace on earth and joy in heaven:
            Christ our God, to you we raise, this our sacrifice of praise.
                                            Words: Folliott S. Pierpoint, 1864, alt.

◆◆◆   5.1.12

Since the following response is in itself a prayer of thanksgiving and dedication, it may be
followed by the Lord's Prayer and a dismissal.

                                                                    HYFRYDOL
God of earth and sea and heaven, by your power all things are made.
We, created in your image, live nor breathe without your aid.
You who formed the earth's wide reaches, summoned forth its fruit and flower,
Teach our hearts to love you only; help us know your grace and power.

You who gave your Son to save us, all our lives to you we owe,
Naught withholding, freely yielding, that the world your love may know.
Now in grateful dedication our allegiance we would own,
Offering talents, time, and treasure, for the mercy you have shown.
                                                Words: Frank Edwards, 1958, alt.

◆◆◆   5.1.13

O God of Bethel, by whose hand your people still are fed,   KINGSFOLD
Who through this earthly pilgrimage our ancestors has led,
Our gifts, our prayers, we now present before your throne of grace,
O God of Jacob, be the God of each succeeding race.
                                    Words: Phillip Doddridge, alt. John Logan, 1781, alt.

PRAYERS OF THANKSGIVING
(when the Eucharist is not celebrated) _____

◆◆◆   5.2.1

Lord God, we rejoice at the promise of your coming,
a promise that awakens us from the night of fear and sin
and sets before us a new day and a new way.

Now send us forth as your Advent people with our minds fixed
on whatever is true and honorable and just and pure and lovely and praiseworthy,
never forgetting that you are near us with your peace. Amen.

◆◆◆　5.2.2

Eternal thanks and praise we offer to you, our God:
For shining the light of your Son Jesus Christ into the darkness of our world,
　　illuminating the hidden places with beams of hope and promise,
For shouting a word into the wilderness of our lives,
　　filling the silent places with words of expectation and joy,
For coming to us and visiting us this day and every day with your presence,
　　forgiving and renewing us to be your people.
For light instead of darkness,
For song instead of silence,
For peace instead of strife,
For presence instead of nothingness,
receive our joyous thanks and praise!

◆◆◆　5.2.3

*No matter which response in the following is sung, no introduction is necessary. The leader
or a vocalist may lead the singing a cappella, or, if there is instrumental accompaniment, a
single note to establish pitch will suffice. It is important that there be no break between the
spoken and sung parts of this prayer.*

Leader:　O God who came in the stillness of the night
　　　　　shattering all human expectations of greatness
　　　　　with the birth of a helpless child,
　　　　　how can we receive this gift of all gifts?
　　　　　How can we comprehend this mystery of all mysteries?
　　　　　Since, O God, we are slow to hear and to see the signs
　　　　　of the new birth of your love,
　　　　　grant us a leading star, that, led to the cradle of grace,
　　　　　we may fall on our knees and offer ourselves
　　　　　in total obedience to the Child of all children.

All:　　　*singing*　　　　　　　　　　　　　　　　　ADESTE FIDELIS
　　　　　Child, for us sinners poor and in the manger,
　　　　　We would embrace you with love and awe;
　　　　　Who would not love you, loving us so dearly?
　　　　　O come, let us adore him,
　　　　　O come, let us adore him,
　　　　　O come, let us adore him, Christ the Lord!
　　　　　　　　Words: John F. Wade, trans. Frederick Oakeley, 1841, alt.

or

FOREST GREEN or ST. LOUIS

O holy Child of Bethlehem! Descend to us, we pray;
Cast out our sin and enter in; be born in us today.
We hear the Christmas angels the great, glad tidings tell;
O come to us, abide with us, our Lord Emmanuel!

Words: Phillips Brooks, 1868

◆◆◆   5.2.4

For renewing the covenant which marks us as your holy people,
For remaking us in the image of your Son, Jesus Christ,
For rekindling in us your Holy Spirit, giving us new life,
To you, God in Three Persons, be honor and glory now and forever!
Amen.

◆◆◆   5.2.5

Minister: Bless the Lord, O my soul;

All: And all that is within me bless God's holy name.

Minister: Bless the Lord, O my soul;

All: And forget not God's benefits.   —Psalm 103:1–2, adapt.

All: Remind us, O God, never to forget:
              never to forget the creative touch of your life-giving hand,
              never to forget the eternal covenant you made
                  with the sons and daughters of Abraham and Sarah,
              never to forget the saving love you gave the world
                  in the life, death, and resurrection of Jesus Christ,
              never to forget the continual outpouring of your Holy Spirit
                  on the church you have gathered.
            Remind us, O God, never to forget, and always to give thanks!

◆◆◆   5.2.6

Eternal God, whose going forth is as sure as the dawn,
we give you thanks for this day and for every day.
We rejoice that your steadfast love greets us every morning,
sustains us throughout each day,
and watches over us when we lie down to sleep.
Remind us of your constant presence,
  that we may offer you the continual thanksgiving of faith and service;
through Jesus Christ our Lord. Amen.

◆◆◆   5.2.7

The following is designed to express in corporate thanksgiving the meaning of 1 Corinthians 12. The four persons presenting the offering may be members of a family, representatives of various groups in the church, or even the ushers who regularly receive the offerings of the people but who rarely lead the prayers.

First person: For the varieties of gifts bestowed on us by the one Spirit,

Second person: For the varieties of service to which we are empowered by one Lord,

Third person: For the varieties of reaching out through which the one God works in us,

Fourth person: For all the unique and precious gifts
the Holy Spirit apportions to each one of us in the body of Christ,

All: **We offer you thanks, O God,
and, united with Christ and one another in baptism,
we commit ourselves to build up the church of Jesus Christ
and to show Christ's love to all the world.**

◆◆◆   5.2.8

**For saying "Yes!" to all of creation and calling it good,
For saying "Yes!" to us in Christ Jesus and sharing our common lot,
For saying "Yes!" to the future and granting us your Holy Spirit,
We offer you, O God, our thankful "Amen!"**

◆◆◆   5.2.9

**God, who so loved the world that you gave your only Son,
we lay before you the offering of ourselves
in joyous thanksgiving for your creating and redeeming love.
Take us and use us in your work of justice and peace.
Lead us as we leave this place, that humbly we may follow you
into the crowded ways of life, there to be instruments of your peace,
in the name of Jesus Christ. Amen.**

"Where Cross the Crowded Ways of Life" is an appropriate hymn to follow this prayer.

◆◆◆   5.2.10

**Thanks be to you, O God, for the healing streams that over us flow,
showering us with your restoring grace, and making us whole again.
Remind us of your constant care, and send us forth into a crying world
with the word and deeds of your perfect peace;
through Jesus Christ our Lord. Amen.**

◆◆◆   5.2.11

For creating us and giving us all that is necessary for life,
For intervening in our foolishness with your judgment and grace,
For refashioning us with the promise of Christlikeness,
For calling us into the household of faith and the body of Christ,
Accept, O God, our feeble attempts at thanks.

◆◆◆   5.2.12

In the following the initial versicle, adapted from the refrain of "We Plow the Fields and Scatter," may be sung by a soloist and congregation as set to the tune WIR PFLÜGEN.

Leader: All good gifts around us are sent from heaven above.

All: **Then thank the Lord, O thank the Lord, for all God's love.**

Leader: For your power that overwhelms us,
           For your grace that assures us,
           For your patience that bears with us,
           For your hope that lifts us up,
           For these and all your gifts,

All: **O generous God, receive our thanks and praise!**

◆◆◆   5.2.13

O vast and wonderful God,
   you are as infinite as the universe, yet as intimate as a touch!
We stand in awe of your world
   and marvel at the intricacies of your creative handiwork.
Your mysteries escape our reasoning and computing,
   yet you surprise us with a holy presence
      wherever two or three are gathered,
   and you assure us that even our inmost thoughts are no secrets to you.
Enable us to approach each moment with a sense of holy reverence,
   to see each person as your precious creation,
   to appreciate each enlargement of mind and senses,
   and to fill each day with joy and hope,
      until at last we are lost in wonder, love, and praise!

An appropriate hymn to follow this prayer is "Love Divine, All Loves Excelling."

◆◆◆ 5.2.14

Triune God, revealed to us in three Persons,
  we remember in joy your countenance turned toward us:
For breathing upon us the creating breath of life,
for freeing us in Christ from bondage to sin and death,
for granting us the empowering gifts of the Spirit,
  receive our thanks and praise.
Send us forth into the days ahead, assured of Christ's promise:
  "I am with you always, to the end of time."

◆◆◆ 5.2.15

The following paraphrase of Psalm 8 may be prayed antiphonally — by pastor and congregation, by congregation and choir, or by two groups within the congregation.

1:      O Lord, our Lord, how glorious is your name in all the earth!

2:      Your glory above the heavens is chanted by the mouths of babes
          and infants.

1:      When we look at the heavens, the work of your fingers,
          at the moon and the stars which you have established,

2:      Who are we that you should at all remember us,
          mere mortals, that you should care for us?

1:      Yet, you have made us little less than the angels,
          and have crowned us with glory and honor!

2:      You have made us master over all your creatures,
          and you have put all things under our feet!

1 & 2: O Lord, our Lord, how glorious is your name in all the earth!

◆◆◆ 5.2.16

O God, who has searched us and known us
  and even numbered the hairs of our heads,
we thank you for telling us again
    that we are infinitely valuable in your sight,
    that we are never separated from your redeeming love,
    and that we are called to be a special people
        with a special mission to a special world you loved so much
        that you gave your only Son, Jesus Christ. Amen.

◆◆◆   5.2.17

We offer you thanks, O compassionate One,
   for your forgiveness far-reaching as the ocean,
   for your grace refreshing and renewing like the dew of the morning,
   for your love made flesh in Jesus Christ and calling us to a joyous rebirth,
   for your hope pushing us to the dawn of a new day.
We give you ourselves, that you will make us instruments
   of a justice extending to all sorts and conditions of humankind,
   of a mercy searching to heal all who hurt in mind and body,
   of a reconciliation reaching out to people of all nations, tongues, and races,
   and of a peace encompassing all the earth.

◆◆◆   5.2.18

The final Gloria Patri *may be sung or spoken in unison. The keyboard accompaniment may
be found on page 208.*

Leader: Know that the Lord who made us is God!

All: **We belong to God; we are God's people,
we are the sheep of God's pasture.**

Leader: Give thanks to God and bless God's name,

All: **For the Lord is good;
God's steadfast love endures forever,
God's faithfulness to all generations.**   —Psalm 100:3, 4b, 5, adapt.

Leader: Eternal praise and thanks we offer to you, our God,

All: **For creating out of nothing every living thing
and supplying every need of your creatures,
For setting free from bondage
the people you have chosen as your very own,
For surprising us with your presence,
surrounding us with your love,
supporting us with your promise,
and raising us up with your power.**

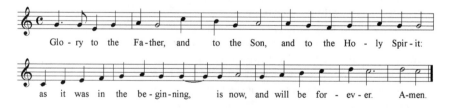

Glo - ry to the Fa - ther, and to the Son, and to the Ho - ly Spir - it:

as it was in the be - gin - ning, is now, and will be for - ev - er. A - men.

Music copyright © 2004 F. Russell Mitman

◆◆◆ 5.2.19

In the following the final phrase, "Lord of all...," may be sung to the final refrain of the hymn "For the Beauty of the Earth" to the tune DIX.

Leader: For our beginning, born in a love that is of God,
            For our becoming, continually measured by the Christ
                and constantly refreshed by the Holy Spirit,
            For our end, promised with life eternal
                by the same love that gave us birth and over and around us lies,

All: Lord of all, to you we raise this our song of thankful praise!

◆◆◆ 5.2.20

The following includes both offertory and dismissal acts. The three verses of Martin Rinkart's hymn, as translated by Catherine Winkworth, are used in such a way that the first verse serves as the offertory response, the second as a corporate blessing, and the third as a concluding doxology. Other inclusive language translations are available and can be used similarly. The prayer of thanksgiving is an adaptation of Psalm 147:10–13, and the doxological part of the blessing is from Ephesians 3:20–21.

Physical movement is an essential part of this act. The offerings of the people are brought to the altar table during the first verse. Following the prayer of thanksgiving, the dismissal begins, and those who brought the offering leave first. If a recessional by choir and other participants is possible, they begin to move out at the beginning of the second verse. The sense of movement out into the world is reinforced by the minister speaking the doxological blessing while walking in the recessional. Following the last verse, all the people leave to be about their vocation in the world. A time for being seated in quiet meditation accompanied by organ chimes would be inappropriate.

All of the above should take place without introduction, directions, or gaps. The keyboard accompanist may want to play through one verse to establish pitch and tempo as the offerings are brought to the altar table. A simple pedal note will suffice to guarantee pitch for the second verse. The last verse may be preceded by an organ interlude, during which a higher key may be established. An instrumental descant may be added, and a resounding amen provides a glorious conclusion.

All: *Standing and singing*   NUN DANKET
            Now thank we all our God with hearts, and hands and voices,
            Who wondrous things has done, in whom the world rejoices,
            Who from our parents' arms has blessed us on our way
            With countless gifts of love, and still is ours today.

The offerings are placed on the altar table.

Leader: All your creatures give thanks to you, O God,

All: And all your people bless you.

Leader: We shall speak of the glory of your realm,

All: **And tell of your power,**

Leader: To make known to all sons and daughters your mighty deeds,

All: **And the glorious splendor of your kingdom.**

Leader: Your reign is everlasting,

All: **And your dominion endures through all generations.**

                                        —Psalm 147:10–13, adapt.

All: *Singing*
          O may this bounteous God through all our life be near us
          With ever joyful hearts and blessed peace to cheer us;
          And keep us in God's grace, and guide us when perplexed,
          And free us from all ills in this world and the next.

Leader: Now to the One who, by all the power at work within us,
          is able to accomplish abundantly far more than all that we ask or imagine,

All: **to God be glory in the church and in Christ Jesus**
          to all generations forever and ever.   —Ephesians 3:20–21, adapt.

All: *Singing*
          All praise and thanks to God who reigns with them in highest heaven,
          to Father and to Son and Spirit now be given,
          The one eternal God, whom heaven and earth adore;
          The God who was, and is, and shall be evermore.

                          Words: Martin Rinkart, 1636, trans. Catherine Winkworth, 1858,
                                        alt. Stanza 3, *Rejoice in the Lord*

Chapter Six

Eucharist

The Christian church stands divided today in large part because of disagreements over what Jesus meant when, in the midst of the Passover meal with his disciples, he took some of the bread, blessed it, broke it, and gave it to them with the promise and injunction, "This is my body, do this in remembrance of me." Luther and the pope argued over *by whom* it is done, Zwingli and Luther fell out over *how* it is done, Calvin and the Zwinglians were at odds over *what* is done, the Elders in Geneva and Calvin disagreed over *when* it should be done, and the Anabaptists questioned *why* it must be done at all. Even the names for the meal reflect a lack of unanimity: Mass, Holy Communion, Lord's Supper, Memorial of the Lord, Divine Liturgy. In this book the word "Eucharist" is used because it appears to be the earliest name of the meal, but the reader is welcome to chose whichever is most comfortable.

Perhaps some of the confusion in definition and terminology results from a misunderstanding that the Eucharist really conjoins three perspectives: a remembrance of the Upper Room supper and Christ's vicarious death, a joyous participation with the risen Christ in a post-Easter meal like the Emmaus road experience, and an eschatological looking ahead to the messianic feast in the heavenly realm. These different dimensions arose out of different traditions in the earliest church, and, according to some scholarship, by the time of Paul they were unified into one act that became the normative experience each Lord's Day. Unlike baptism, which is a one-time act, we do this act — literally, "make Eucharist" — repeatedly, that in this doing and making, Christ is at one with the church in a sacramental communion effected by God through the Holy Spirit. *How* all this takes place I shall leave for others to debate. From the New Testament and other early Christian sources we learn that the Eucharist as we know it today began as a communal meal. Paul's reminder to the Corinthians about its sacred institution at the Passover supper (1 Cor. 11–17ff.) reveals that it apparently had been normative for the church to share a *koinonia* meal in which they celebrated the presence of the risen Christ and looked forward to his imminent return. The rubrics of the ancient church manual called the *Didache* reveal further that this meal was preceded and followed by prayers of thanksgiving: in other words, by table graces before and after dinner. It is from that basic setting that all liturgies for the Eucharist ancient and modern have evolved.

The structure of the liturgical action in the meal developed from the action of Jesus' institution at the Passover supper: "Now as they were eating, Jesus *took* bread, and *blessed* it, and *broke* it, and *gave* it to the disciples and said, 'Take, eat; this is my body'" (Matt. 26:26, emphasis added). These four actions: *take, bless, break, give,* together with the post-meal thanksgiving, became the structure of the Eucharist. They are also the criteria in our creation of liturgical expressions for the celebration of this sacramental act.

The injunction to *take* is utilitarian. The meal needs to be prepared, and the table needs to be set. This is the reason, as was said earlier, for the offertory to be part of the Eucharist itself. It is the time when the elements are brought to the altar table and the preparations made. It is the time also for us to prepare ourselves to be the guests, and it may even be the time for us to come physically to the table. The action of preparation can be emphasized by the movements associated with bringing the elements to the table or, if that is impossible, by uncovering the elements. Representative persons from the congregation or those who will assist in the distribution may present the gifts of the elements along with the offerings (both money and other gifts) of the people.

The second aspect (*bless*) is giving thanks, the grace before the meal. Usually it is designated as the Eucharistic prayer. It may be prefaced by an exchange of greetings and the peace as well as by the traditional *Sursum corda* ("lift up your hearts"). Essentially the Eucharistic prayer begins with a remembering (*anamnesis*) of God's saving deeds in history and of Christ's life, death, and resurrection. It looks ahead also to the fulfillment at the end of time and the messianic banquet of which each meal is a foretaste. Finally, it asks God to accept us — now — as guests at the table and, through the Holy Spirit, to bless the bread and wine we offer together with our thanksgiving, that Christ will be at one with us in the meal. This prayer, sometimes called the Great Prayer, is not only a prayer but also an affirmation of faith and a hymn of praise. Often it may include the singing or shouting of praise in the *Sanctus* ("Holy, holy, holy") and the *Benedictus* ("Blessed is the one who comes"). A number of the great hymns of the church, both historic and contemporary, are appropriately used within the Eucharistic prayer. Or, depending on the setting, it may take the form of a simple yet joyous table grace that may be said or sung in unison.

The *breaking* of the bread and the pouring of the cup are the third part of the Eucharistic act. In some liturgies the words of institution are said as accompaniment to the manual acts of breaking and pouring; in others the words are part of the Eucharistic prayer, and separate words are used with the manual acts. In either case, the powerful nonverbal symbols of breaking and pouring should never be eliminated. They are as important as the words. Since, according to the one tradition that Paul says he received and passed on, the institution occurred in the midst of the Passover meal, it may be fitting, depending on the setting, to break *and* distribute the bread in a unified act and then to pour *and* distribute the cup as another unified act. Interestingly, in the tradition preserved in the *Didache,* the cup comes before the bread.

The fourth action is the distribution (*give*), and there are a number of ways by which the distribution may take place. Pew Communion with individual glasses was the twentieth-century redaction of the early Zwinglian and Anglican custom of sitting in the pews to receive Communion. However, there are other valid methods. Luther, Calvin, and the French and German Reformed churches followed the early church's practice of having people stand around the table. The Scottish and Dutch Reformed preferred sitting at tables in remembrance of the Last Supper. Kneeling was reintroduced by later Anglicans and continued by Wesley. It seems to me that the number of persons communing and the physical setting of the worship space should be the determining factors in how the elements are served. What is important is that Communion be a communal meal as much as possible. Therefore, the coffin-like altars that were nailed to chancel's back walls during the Romantic era and that were baptized as normative by the twentieth century's aesthetic approach to worship are really out of place. Altars with priests facing the wall and their backs to the people were the result of the process of clerical withdrawal that took place around the ninth century. Neither the early church, nor the Reformers of the sixteenth century, nor even Vatican II of the twentieth century could tolerate such separation of table from people. Interestingly, every Roman Catholic church in the decades since Vatican II has installed a table facing the people for the Eucharist. Calvin did the same thing in the sixteenth century.

During the distribution and Communion there are a variety of accompaniments possible and appropriate. The simplest is silence, allowing the nonverbal acts of receiving, eating, and drinking together to speak for themselves. Another method with historical precedents is the reading of appropriate selections of Scripture during distribution of the elements. Still another is congregational singing of hymns or psalms during distribution and, if communicants come to the altar table, even during the administration. Two cautions seem to be in order. The first is a reminder that whatever the accompaniment, it is neither "mood" nor "cover-up" music to mask the movement. It seems strange to me that we Americans often carpet our churches to cover up the sound of people's footsteps! Movement is symbolically important and needs no artificial devices. The second caution is an exhortation to let the accompaniment reflect that this is indeed a Eucharist (literally, "joyous thanksgiving") and not a lugubrious and funereal rite. The Eucharist recalls Christ's death, yes, but a death seen through the glory of Easter's resurrection and the hope of *Maranatha*.

Following the Communion the Eucharistic act concludes, like the act of baptism, with a brief thanksgiving. Our at-one-ness with Christ has been accomplished by sacramental grace, and we are moved to say our last words of thanks before we get up from the table and go into the world, where Christ will meet us in many disguises. Sometimes the post-communion prayer is, together with our thanksgiving, a request for the Holy Spirit to strengthen us and to commission us to be about Christ's work as a holy people. On other occasions, the sending forth may take the form of a charge as part of the concluding act. We shall discuss this in the next chapter.

There are differences in traditions as to who presides at Eucharist. In some churches only those ordained may officiate, while in others there is no differentiation made. In the following I use "minister" to designate the person who presides in the liturgy with the understanding that the "minister" may or may not be ordained according to the tradition in which these liturgies are used.

LITURGIES FOR THE EUCHARIST _____

◆◆◆ 6.1.1

In the following liturgy for Advent Eucharist the hymn stanzas may serve as the offertory response while the elements are brought to the table.

All: *Singing*   WINCHESTER NEW
      On Jordan's bank the Baptist's cry announces that the Lord is nigh;
      Awake and hearken, for he brings glad tidings of the King of kings!

      Then cleansed be every life from sin;
      make straight the way for God within.
      And let us all our hearts prepare for Christ to come and enter there.

Minister: Lift up your hearts!

All: **We lift them to the Lord!**

Minister: Let us give thanks to God,

All: **For the Lord is good, and God's love is everlasting.**

Minister: We thank you, O God, that from the very beginning
           your Word has been the light and life of the world.
           Through your Word all things were made,
           and by your Word we shall be made new.

All: **Come, Lord Jesus!**

Minister: We remember that in every age
           you have called patriarchs and prophets, apostles and martyrs
           to bear witness to the light of your Word,
           that all people may believe.

All: **Come, Lord Jesus!**

Minister: We rejoice that your Word became flesh and dwelt among us,
           full of grace and truth,
           and that, beholding the incarnation of your glory,
           we all have received grace upon grace.

All: **Come, Lord Jesus!**

Minister: We remember that by becoming flesh of our flesh,
           Christ sanctified all of life from birth to death,
           and to redeem us he took upon himself
           the whole range of our human existence.

All: **Christ was born, Christ has died, Christ has risen,**
      and Christ will come again!

Minister: Through the powerful benediction of your Holy Spirit
we ask you to come and to transform us
and these gifts of bread and wine
that we offer with our praise and thanksgiving,
that we may be fed with these holy mysteries
and be so united with Christ
until we finally eat at his table in the heavenly realm.

All: **Amen. Come, Lord Jesus!**

The minister repeats the words of institution in the customary manner, breaks the bread, and pours the cup. All pray the Lord's Prayer, and the Communion may be distributed with appropriate words of administration. After all have received, the service continues with the following prayer of thanksgiving:

Minister: In Bethlehem, the place of bread, you came, O Jesus,
incarnated in the body of a helpless child
and wrapped in the diapers of our own common humanity
to be fully God with us.

All: **Come again, Emmanuel!**

Minister: At the Bethlehem of this table you have come to us today
in the midst of a common meal of everyday bread and wine
to feed us with mysteries beyond our imagining.

All: **Come again, O Bread of Life!**

Minister: To the Bethlehems of this world where there is no peace
and holy places are desecrated by the machines of violence,
and people yearn for just a morsel of heaven,

All: **Come again, Lord Jesus! Come!**

The service may continue with the singing of "Come, O Long-expected Jesus."

◆◆◆ 6.1.2

The following is designed as a liturgy for Christmas Eve Eucharist. In an intimate setting, the congregation may come to the table during the offertory, make their offering, and then remain gathered around the table for the remainder of the service. During the offertory a solo voice and congregation may sing antiphonally "What Child Is This?" or, also antiphonally or in unison, "Angels We Have Heard on High." The hymn text included may be sung to ST. LOUIS *or* FOREST GREEN.

Minister: Lift up your hearts!

All: **We lift them to the Lord!**

Minister: O God of wonder, we come to this table
to be surrounded by the mystery of heaven's radiance.
Lift us from the ordinary,
that we may be touched by things extraordinary this night,
and with the choirs of angels join in praising:

All: **Glory to God in the highest heaven,
and on earth peace, goodwill among all people!** —Luke 2:14, adapt.

Minister: We praise you for coming to humankind in ways we humans can grasp,
for being born Child for all children,
and living as the human One for all humankind,
that all people may be redeemed through him.

All: **For a child has been born for us, a son given to us;
authority rests upon his shoulders; and he is named
Wonderful Counselor, Mighty God,
Everlasting Father, Prince of Peace.** —Isaiah 9:6

Minister: We thank you that by his death on the cross
and through the triumph of his resurrection
we are privileged to share now in the new life of his realm
and at last to be united in the glorious company of all the saints.

All: **And the Word became flesh and lived among us,
and we have seen his glory, the glory as of a father's only son,
full of grace and truth.** —John 1:14

Singing:
**O Holy Child of Bethlehem, descend to us, we pray.
Cast out our sin, and enter in, be born in us today.
We hear the Christmas angels the great glad tidings tell.
O come to us, abide with us, our Lord Emmanuel.**
Words: Phillips Brooks, 1868

*The minister breaks the bread and pours the cup accompanied by the words of institution.
All pray the Lord's Prayer. During the distribution the birth narrative (Luke 2:1–20) may
be read or the congregation may sing a series of carols that proclaim the nativity message.
Following the distribution, congregational candles may be lighted and all pray the following
prayer of thanksgiving.*

All: **We thank you, O God, for feeding us with holy mysteries
that assure us of your being at one with us.
Grant that the angels' song may be continually on our lips
and Christ's light may radiate in our lives,**

that we may bear the good news of your love
to a dark and waiting world.

*The service may end with the singing of "Go, Tell It on the Mountain," and the congregation
may carry their candles outside the church.*

◆◆◆   6.1.3

*The following liturgy is especially appropriate for the season of Epiphany and for occasions
when baptism is celebrated or remembered. Persons celebrating anniversaries of their baptisms
may present the elements. The concluding* Gloria Patri *(Glory to the Father) may be sung.
A musical setting may be found on page 208.*

Minister: O God, who has called us from darkness into light,
            we remember your eternal promise to lead your people
            from the shadows of bondage to freedom's new dawning.
            We recall how in the fullness of time
            you gave us yourself in Christ Jesus, the light of the world.
            We thank you that by the power of your Holy Spirit
            we are born again in baptism as children of light.
            We recall that on the eve of darkness, on the night he was betrayed,
            Jesus took bread, and when he had blessed it, he broke it,
            and gave it to his disciples, saying,
            "Take, eat, this is my body, broken for you."
            And, after supper he took the cup, saying,
            "This cup is the new testament in my blood.
            Do this, as often as you drink it, in remembrance of me."
            We rejoice that on the day of resurrection,
            when he was at table with two of the disciples,
            he took the bread, blessed and broke it, and gave it to them.
            And their eyes were opened, and they recognized him.

            At the institution, and upon the promise of our Lord Jesus Christ,
            we celebrate this joyous feast
            and join with the holy church throughout all the world in praising you.

All: *Singing or speaking*   NICAEA
            Holy, holy, holy! God the Almighty!
            All your works shall praise your name in earth and sky and sea;
            Holy, holy, holy! Merciful and mighty!
            God in three persons, blessed Trinity!

                                              Words: Reginald Heber, 1826, alt.

Minister: By the presence of your Holy Spirit may these gifts we offer
            be transformed from ordinary to holy things,
            so that as we eat and drink of them at this table,
            we may be fed and nourished with the body and blood of Christ,

and so be united with him until we shall feast face to face
at the glorious banquet table of heaven.

Minister: *Breaking the bread*
The bread which we break
is a means of sharing in the body of Christ.

Pouring the cup
The cup of blessing we bless
is a means of sharing in the blood of Christ.

All: **For every time we eat this bread and drink the cup,
we proclaim the death of the Lord until he comes.**

All pray the Lord's Prayer.

Minister: Take and eat; this is the body of Christ which is broken for you.

Minister: This cup is the new covenant in the blood of Christ shed for you.

The act may conclude with the singing of the Nunc Dimittis *and the* Gloria Patri *or the
following responsive version.*

Minister: Lord, now let your servants depart in peace,
according to your word,

All: **For our eyes have seen the salvation
you have prepared in the sight of all people:**

Minister: A light to reveal you to the nations,

All: **And the glory of your people Israel.**   —Luke 2:29–32, adapt.

Minister: Glory to the Father, and to the Son, and to the Holy Spirit;

All: **As it was in the beginning, is now, and ever shall be,
world without end. Amen.**

◆◆◆ 6.1.4

*The following Eucharistic liturgy is designed for use either on Ash Wednesday or on the First
Sunday in Lent. With the substitution of another hymn, it may be used during Holy Week.
The initial hymn verses may serve as the offertory response, and, depending on the number
of persons present, the congregation may gather around the table or at the rail during the
singing.*

All: *Singing*   ST. FLAVIAN
**Lord Jesus, who through forty days for us did fast and pray,
Teach us with you to mourn our sins, and close by you to stay.**

As you with Satan did contend and did the victory win,
O give us strength to persevere, in you to conquer sin.

Words: Claudia F. I. Hernaman, 1873, alt.

Minister: Let us approach this table in true penitence and contrition.

All: **We come to this your table, O Lord,
in company with tax collectors and sinners.
We acknowledge that we are not worthy to partake of this holy meal.
Yet, on the promise of our Lord Jesus Christ,
we come to be forgiven and to be made whole again.
Grant that as we eat this bread and drink this cup,
we may be at one with Christ
in his pilgrimage to the cross to die with him.
And, when "He is risen" greets Easter's morn,
may we also be raised with him to new life. Amen.**

Minister: Lift up your hearts!

All: **We lift them up to the Lord!**

Minister: Let us give thanks:

Minister: For your creating hand that brought the worlds into being
and fashions every living thing,
and for stretching your holy arm
to bring your people in every generation from bondage to freedom:

All: **Receive our thanks, O God.**

Minister: For coming to us in Jesus our Lord,
sharing our human lot, suffering and dying for us,
and being raised that we, too, may share in resurrection life:

All: **Receive our praise, O God.**

Minister: For the outpouring of your Holy Spirit,
calling and empowering the church
with an abundance of spiritual gifts:

All: **Receive, O God, our offering of thanksgiving and praise.**

Spoken antiphonally or sung in unison to OLD HUNDREDTH:

Minister: Be present at our table, Lord!

All: **Be here and everywhere adored!**

Minister: Bless now this bread and wine we share,

All: **And for heaven's banquet us prepare.**

Minister: *Breaking the bread*
 The Lord Jesus on the night when he was betrayed took bread,
 and when he had given thanks, he broke it, and said,
 "This is my body which is broken for you.
 Do this in remembrance of me."

 Pouring the cup
 In the same way also the cup, after supper, saying,
 "This cup is the new covenant in my blood.
 Do this, as often as you drink it, in remembrance of me."

Minister: Behold the Lamb of God who takes away the sin of the world!

All: **Our Father . . .**

During the distribution, the minister or reader(s) may read without references Isaiah 53:4–6
and John 4:9–11.

Minister: For broken bread and outpoured wine,
 signs of your life given and poured out in love
 for us and for all humankind, we give you thanks, O Christ.

All: *Singing*   ST. FLAVIAN
 Lord, through these days of penitence, and through your Passiontide,
 Yes, evermore, in life and death, Jesus, with us abide.

 Abide with us, that so, this life of suffering over-past
 An Easter of unending joy we may attain at last!
                                          Words: Claudia F. I. Hernaman, 1873, alt.

◆◆◆ 6.1.5

A magnificent hymn attributed to Bernard of Clairvaux provides the framework for con-
gregational response in the following. Although this liturgy is particularly appropriate for
the Lenten season, it also may be used on other occasions when the tone at the service is
quiet and reflective. The hymn is set to a number of tunes, and one may choose the tune
most familiar to the worshipers. The initial stanzas may serve as the offertory response dur-
ing which the communion elements may be brought to the altar/table. The first three lines,
"O Jesus . . . imparts," may be sung by a soloist or the celebrant with the congregation joining
to sing the last line, "We turn, unfilled, to hear your call."

The liturgy may be adapted for use in settings where there are no printed bulletins. Then
all that is needed for the congregation are hymnals or printed sheets with the words to the
hymn stanzas; and the singing may be done a cappella or with guitar, autoharp, or similar
accompaniment. No elaborate instructions are necessary. The leader or officiant may begin
singing, and the congregation will follow.

O Jesus, joy of loving hearts,
The fount of life, the light of all:
From every bliss that earth imparts
We turn, unfilled, to hear your call.

Your truth unchanged has ever stood;
You save all those who on you call
To those who seek you, you are good;
To those who find you, all in all.

For you our restless spirits yearn,
Wherever our changing lot is cast;
Glad, when your smile on us you turn,
Blessed, when by faith we hold you fast.

Minister: We remember, O God, your eternal decision for us
and for the whole world in the death and resurrection of Jesus,
your Son, our Lord and Christ.

We give thanks that you have called us to this table
to be united with him in his passion and victory
and to share with each other the sorrows and joys of his church on earth.

We ask you to come among us with your Holy Spirit
and to bless us and these gifts of bread and wine,
that we may be fed with these holy mysteries
until we feast face to face with Christ and the whole company of the saints
in your heavenly realm.

We offer you ourselves — heart, soul, mind, and strength —
asking you to accept this living sacrifice of our praise and thanksgiving
for Christ's one offering of himself for us.

All: *Singing*
We taste you, ever-living bread,
And long to feast upon you still;
We drink of you, the fountainhead;
Our thirsty souls from you we fill.

The words of institution may be joined with the manual acts of breaking the bread and pouring the cup, followed by the Lord's Prayer. During the distribution the words of institution may be repeated, or other appropriate words of administration may be used. After all have communed, the service continues with the following thanksgiving:

Minister: Lord Jesus, thank you for your presence here
to feed us with simple things that sign your intimacy with us.
Send us from this table to the places where you are calling us
to feed a hungering and thirsty world.

All: *Singing*
     O Jesus, ever with us stay!
     Make all our moments fair and bright!
     Oh, chase the night of sin away!
     Shed o'er the world your holy light.

◆◆◆   6.1.6

In the following the offertory hymn and response are included. During the singing of the hymn stanzas the communion elements may be brought to the table along with the offerings of the people. In services in which the Eucharist is not celebrated, this same act through the hymn stanza "What language shall I borrow . . . " may be used as an offertory response and accompanying prayer of thanksgiving.

OFFERTORY HYMN: *The congregation may stand.*   PASSION CHORALE

     O Jesus, we adore you, upon the cross, our King!
     We bow our hearts before you, your gracious name we sing.
     That name has brought salvation, that name in life our stay,
     Our peace, our consolation, when life shall fade away.

     Yet still the world contemns you, still passing by the cross;
     Lord, may our hearts retain you, all else we count but loss.
     Ah, Lord, our sins arraigned you, and nailed you to the tree;
     Our pride, our Lord, disdained you, yet deign our hope to be.
                                   Words: Arthur T. Russell, 1851, alt.

Minister: Lift up your hearts!

All: We lift them up to the Lord!

Minister: Lord Jesus Christ, who in self-sacrificing love
           poured out yourself on the cross for us,

All: We offer you our worship and devotion.

Minister: Lord Jesus Christ, who in sin-conquering love
           opened to us the resurrection and the life,

All: We offer you our thanks and praise.

Minister: Lord Jesus Christ, who in world-redeeming love
           reigns over all and seeks in love to draw us and all people to yourself.

All: We offer you our faith and service.

All: *Singing* PASSION CHORALE
What language shall we borrow to thank you, dearest Friend,
For all your dying sorrow, your pity without end?
O keep us near you ever, and should we perish too,
Lord, let us never, never, outlive our love for you.

> Words: Medieval Latin, attrib. to Bernard of Clairvaux (1091–1153),
> German paraphrase by Paul Gerhardt, 1656,
> translated by James W. Alexander, 1830, alt.

Minister: With language borrowed only from angelic choirs,
yet mirrored dimly in the distortions of human words,
we attempt to express our gratitude, Lord Jesus,
for the gift of your wondrous love for us.
Through the Word you were from the beginning,
and in you all things have come into being.
In you was life, and the life was the light of all people.
Born of Mary, you became the Word made flesh,
dwelling among us, full of grace and truth.
Dying at the hands of your accusers, you were raised in glory,
and from your fullness have we all received grace upon grace.
Therefore, we join with all on earth who name your name,
and all who surround you in heaven, to sing our praise:

All: *Singing* PASSION CHORALE
O Glorious Christ, we bless you and with the angels cry:
O Jesus, we confess you the Son enthroned on high!
Lord, grant our sins remission; life through your death restore,
And grant us the fruition of life forevermore.

> Words: Arthur Russell, 1851, adapt.

Minister: Bless us and these gifts of bread and wine, that, now being set apart
from a common to a sacred and mystical use
they may represent to us your body and your blood,
and that through the power of the Holy Spirit,
we may be made to partake really and truly of your blessed life.

All: Lord Jesus Christ, open our eyes that we too may see you
in the breaking of this bread!

Minister: Great is the mystery of faith:

All: Christ has died. Christ is risen. Christ will come again.

*Intercessions may be included here. The minister breaks the bread and pours the cup together
with the accompanying words of institution. All pray the Lord's Prayer.*

Minister: Behold the Lamb of God who takes away the sin of the world!
Come, for all things are ready.

The elements are served. After all have communed, the service continues with the following thanksgiving:

All: Lord Jesus Christ, we thank you for giving yourself for us
          and for satisfying our hunger with this eucharistic food.
        Send us forth in the reconciling and healing peace of the cross
          to walk in the light and believe in the light
          that we and all people may become the children of light;
          through our Lord Jesus Christ, the Light of the world. Amen

The hymn "Lift High the Cross" may follow.

◆◆◆ 6.1.7

The following is an order for Eucharist on Palm/Passion Sunday or Maundy Thursday. It continues the passion narrative in Matthew 26:17–27:54 and is a complement to the combined gathering and penitential act at number 2.1.18.. The hymn stanzas may be sung a cappella. The keyboard accompaniments may be found on pages 210 and 211. The final stanza, as printed, may be sung in the major key.

Leader 1: On the first day of Unleavened Bread the disciples came to Jesus, saying, "Where do you want us to make the preparations for you to eat the Passover?"

Leader 2: "Go into the city to a certain man, and say to him, 'The Teacher says, My time is near; I will keep the Passover at your house with my disciples.'"

Leader 1: So the disciples did as Jesus had directed them, and they prepared the Passover meal.

The bread and wine may be brought to the altar/table.

All: *Singing*   MAUNDY

It hap-pened on that dread-ful night when powers of earth and hell a-rose
a-gainst the Son, our God's de-light, and friends be-trayed him to his foes.

Minister: *(or soloist) singing, while the minister breaks the bread:*   MAUNDY
         Before the bitter scene began,
           he took the bread, and blessed and broke.
         What love through all his actions ran!
           What wondrous words of love he spoke!

> "My body, broken for your sin,
>   receive and eat as living food."

Minister: *(or soloist) continues singing, while the minister pours the cup:*
>   He took the cup and blessed the wine:
>   "Share this new testament, my blood."

Minister: *(or soloist)*
>   "Do this," he said, "till time shall end,
>   remembering your dying friend;
>   Meet at my table and record
>   the full obedience of your Lord."

All: *Singing*   MAUNDY

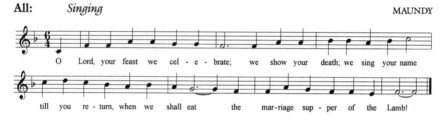

O Lord, your feast we cel - e - brate; we show your death; we sing your name till you re - turn, when we shall eat the mar-riage sup - per of the Lamb!

Hymn stanzas: Isaac Watts, 1709, alt.; Music: F. Russell Mitman, 2004

Intercessions may be offered followed by the Lord's Prayer. During the distribution of the elements the hymn "Go to Dark Gethsemane" may be sung.

Leader 1: When they had sung the hymn, they went out to the Mount of Olives. Then Jesus said to them,

Leader 2: "You will all become deserters because of me this night. . . . But after I am raised up, I will go ahead of you to Galilee."

Leader 1: Peter said to him, "Though all become deserters because of you, I will never desert you." Jesus said to him,

Leader 2: "Truly I tell you, this very night, before the cock crows, you will deny me three times."

Leader 1: Peter said to him, "Even though I must die with you, I will not deny you." And so said all the disciples.

Silence

Leader 1: Then Jesus went with them to a place called Gethsemane; and he said to his disciples,

Leader 2: "Sit here while I go over there and pray."

Leader 1: He took with him Peter and the two sons of Zebedee, and began to be grieved and agitated. Then he said to them,

Leader 2: "I am deeply grieved, even to death; remain here, and stay awake with me."

Silence

Leader 1: And going a little farther, he threw himself on the ground and prayed,

Leader 2: "My Father, if it is possible, let this cup pass from me; yet not what I want but what you want."

Silence

Leader 1: Then he came to the disciples and found them sleeping; and he said to Peter,

Leader 2: "So, could you not stay awake with me one hour? Stay awake and pray that you may not come into the time of trial; the spirit indeed is willing, but the flesh is weak."

Silence

Leader 1: Again he went away for the second time and prayed,

Leader 2: "My Father, if this cannot pass unless I drink it, your will be done."

Silence

Leader 1: Again he came and found them sleeping, for their eyes were heavy. So leaving them again, he went away and prayed for the third time, saying the same words. Then he came to the disciples and said to them,

Leader 2: "Are you still sleeping and taking your rest? See, the hour is at hand, and the Son of Man is betrayed into the hands of sinners. Get up, let us be going. See, my betrayer is at hand!"

The reading of the narrative continues with Matthew 26:46–27:10, followed by:

Leader 1: Jesus stood before the governor; and the governor asked him, "Are you the King of the Jews?" Jesus said,

Leader 2: "You say so."

Leader 1: But when he was accused by the chief priests and elders, he did not answer. Then Pilate said to him, "Do you not hear how many accusations they make against you?" But he gave him no answer, not even to a single charge, so that the governor was greatly amazed.

Leader 1: Now at the festival the governor was accustomed to release a prisoner for the crowd, anyone whom they wanted. At that time they had a notorious prisoner called Jesus Barabbas. So after they had gathered, Pilate said to them, "Whom do you want me to release for you, Jesus Barabbas or Jesus who is called the Messiah?"... While he was sitting on the judgment seat, his wife sent word to him, "Have nothing to do with that innocent man, for today I have suffered a great deal because of a dream about him." Now the chief priests and the elders persuaded the crowds to ask for Barabbas and to have Jesus killed. The governor again said to them, "Which of the two do you want me to release for you?"

All: *Shouting*
"Barabbas!"

Leader 1: "Then what should I do with Jesus who is called the Messiah?"

All: *Shouting*
"Let him be crucified!"

Leader 1: "Why, what evil has he done?"

All: *Shouting*
"Let him be crucified!"

Leader 1: So when Pilate saw that he could do nothing, but rather that a riot was beginning, he took some water and washed his hands before the crowd, saying, "I am innocent of this man's blood; see to it yourselves." Then the people as a whole answered,

All: **"His blood be on us and on our children!"**

Leader 1: So he released Barabbas for them; and after flogging Jesus, he handed him over to be crucified.

The narration continues with Matthew 27:27–44, followed by:

Leader 1: From noon on, darkness came over the whole land until three in the afternoon. And about three o'clock Jesus cried with a loud voice,

Leader 2: "Eli, Eli, lema sabachthani?"
"My God, my God, why have you forsaken me?"

Leader 1: When some of the bystanders heard it, they said, "This man is calling for Elijah." At once one of them ran and got a sponge, filled it with sour wine, put it on a stick, and gave it to him to drink. But the others said, "Wait, let us see whether Elijah will come to save him." Then Jesus cried again with a loud voice and breathed his last. At that moment the curtain of the temple was torn in two, from top to bottom. The earth shook, and the rocks were split. Now when the centurion and those with him, who were keeping watch over Jesus, saw the earthquake and what took place, they were terrified and said, "Truly this man was a son of God!"

All: *Singing*   PASSION CHORALE

Lord, be my consolation; shield me when I must die;
Remind me of your passion when my last hour draws nigh.
These eyes, new faith receiving, from you shall never move;
Whoever dies believing dies safely in your love.

Words: attrib. Bernard of Clairvaux;
par. Paul Gerhardt, 1656; trans. James W. Alexander, 1830, alt.

Please be dismissed in silence.

◆◆◆   6.1.8

The following order is for the celebration of the Eucharist on Easter, joining the words of Jesus' Last Supper with Christ's Easter peace-greeting and the account of Christ's encounter with the disciples on the Emmaus road. The word "Lord" in the Sursum Corda *("Lift up your hearts") refers to the risen Christ. The act begins immediately following the offertory response. The joyous hymn stanzas can be enhanced with choral or instrumental descants.*

Minister: The peace of our Lord Jesus Christ be with you.

All: And also with you.

All may greet one another with "Peace be with you" or another Easter greeting.

Minister: Lift up your hearts!

All: We lift them up to the Lord!

Minister: We praise you, O Christ, for your resurrection triumph
over the powers of sin and death,
assuring us that, because you live we shall live also
and that nothing can separate us from your love.

All: Thanks be to you for giving us the victory!

Minister: We remember your Passover communion with those gathered
at table with you and recall your Easter encounter
in the breaking of the bread with those you met
on the road to Emmaus.

All: Thanks be to you for giving us the victory!

Minister: We rejoice in the dawning of the new life you promise the world,
offering hope to the hopeless and voice to the voiceless,
justice to those who suffer injustice
and peace to those who know no peace,
health to those who have no health and love for those who have no love.

All: Thanks be to you for giving us the victory!

Minister: We offer you these gifts, a sacrifice of our praise and thanksgiving,
praying that as we eat and drink at this joyous feast of the resurrection,
our eyes too may be opened,
and we, too, may know you with us in the breaking of this bread.

All: *Singing*
Hail, the Lord of earth and heaven! Alleluia!
Praise to you, by both be given! Alleluia!
Every knee to you shall bow, Alleluia!
Risen Christ, triumphant now! Alleluia!

Minister: The Lord Jesus, on the night before he died,
While they were eating, took a loaf of bread, and after blessing it
broke it, gave it to them, and said, "Take; this is my body."
Then Jesus took a cup, and, after giving thanks, gave it to them,
and all of them drank from it.
Jesus said to them, "This is my blood of the new covenant,
which is poured out for many.
Truly I tell you,
I will never again drink of the fruit of the vine until that day
when I drink it new in the kingdom of God."   —Mark 14:22-25, alt.

Minister: Great is the mystery of faith:

All: **Christ has died,**
Christ is risen,
Christ will come again.

Intercessions may be included, and all pray the Lord's Prayer.

Minister: *Breaking the bread*
In the breaking of the bread
we are at one with Christ in his death and resurrection.

Pouring the cup
Through the cup of blessing we share in the new life
Christ pours out for the world.
Come, for all things are ready!

During distribution Luke 24:33–49a may be read. While the assembly are receiving or after all have received the bread and cup, the minister may say the following words, which are adapted from Calvin's Communion liturgy:

Minister: May Jesus, the true Savior of the world,
who died for us and is seated in glory,
dwell in your hearts through the Holy Spirit,
that you may be wholly alive in Christ,
through living faith and perfect love.

After all have communed the minister gives thanks:

Minister: Thanks be to God who gives us the victory
            through our Lord Jesus Christ!

All: *Singing*
            Soar we now, where Christ has led, Alleluia!
            Following our exalted Head, Alleluia!
            Made like him, like him we rise, Alleluia!
            Ours the cross, the grave, the skies, Alleluia!

                                            Hymn stanzas: Charles Wesley, 1739 alt.

◆◆◆ 6.1.9

*The following is designed for a celebration of Eucharist on Easter Evening or on the Third
Sunday of Easter in Lectionary Year A. It also is appropriate for any celebration of the mission
of the church. The following reading of the Emmaus Road encounter is best accomplished by
three readers, two male and one female. It begins before the offertory. The suggestion that the
table be spread with a linen cloth is a significant symbolic action reflecting the linen cloths
that were found in the tomb on Easter morning.*

Leader 1:   Two of the disciples were going to a village called Emmaus, about seven
            miles from Jerusalem, and talking with each other about all these things
            that had happened. While they were talking and discussing, Jesus himself
            came near and went with them, but their eyes were kept from recognizing
            him. And he said to them,

Leader 2:   "What are you discussing with each other while you walk along?"

Leader 1:   They stood still, looking sad. Then one of them, whose name was Cleopas,
            answered him,

Leader 3:   "Are you the only stranger in Jerusalem who does not know the things
            that have taken place there in these days?"

Leader 2:   "What things?"

Leader 3:   "The things about Jesus of Nazareth, who was a prophet mighty in deed
            and word before God and all the people, and how our chief priests and
            leaders handed him over to be condemned to death and crucified him.
            But we had hoped that he was the one to redeem Israel. Yes, and besides
            all this, it is now the third day since these things took place. Moreover,
            some women of our group astounded us. They were at the tomb early
            this morning, and when they did not find his body there, they came back
            and told us that they had indeed seen a vision of angels who said that he
            was alive. Some of those who were with us went to the tomb and found
            it just as the women had said; but they did not see him."

Leader 2: "Oh, how foolish you are, and how slow of heart to believe all that the prophets have declared! Was it not necessary that the Messiah should suffer these things and then enter into his glory?"

Leader 1: Then beginning with Moses and all the prophets, he interpreted to them the things about himself in all the Scriptures. As they came near the village to which they were going, he walked ahead as if he were going on. But they urged him strongly, saying,

Leader 3: "Stay with us, because it is almost evening and the day is now nearly over."

Leader 1: So he went in to stay with them.   —Luke 24:13–29, adapt.

During the offering a choir or the congregation may sing the hymn "Stay with Us," words by Herbert Brokering, music by Walter L. Pelz. A linen cloth may be carried in and spread on the altar table followed by the communion elements.

Minister: When Christ was at table with them, he took bread and blessed and broke it, and gave it to them, and their eyes were opened, and they recognized him.

All: **In company with all believers in every time and beyond time, we gather at this table to know the risen Christ in the breaking of the bread.**
    —*Service of Word and Sacrament II,* copyright 1969, United Church Press, adapt.

Minister: Lift up your hearts!

All: **We lift them to God in praise and thanksgiving!**

Minister: Holy God, all creation is your handiwork,
    and all creatures are precious in your sight.
    The vastness of the universe is beyond our imagining and computing,
    yet you invade our hearts with a wondrous intimacy
    that burns deep within each solitary soul.

    You surprised our ancestors, Abraham and Sarah, through strangers
    who met them in their desert fears with words of promise and blessing.

    In Jesus Christ you became flesh, unknown but to shepherds and angels,
    and you surprised a world waiting for a warrior by dying in powerlessness.

    In Jesus you touched human brokenness:
    the sightless began to see, the deaf to hear, the lame to walk,
    the imprisoned to be free, the fearful to trust, the faithless to believe.

    In Christ crucified you bore alone the pain of isolation and rejection,
    destroyed the powers of sin and death,
    and welcomed into paradise those dying with you.

In Christ resurrected you came to Mary in the guise of a gardener
and broke bread with disciples as a stranger joining them on the road.

Through the Holy Spirit foreign tongues from every nation
amazingly began to speak with one voice,
and people who were aliens and once far off were brought near,
made citizens with the saints
and numbered with prophets and apostles.

Through the Holy Spirit the church was empowered:
the broken made whole,
the strangers welcomed,
the silent given a word to speak,
and the empty filled with good things.

Therefore, we praise you, O God, joining our voices
with choirs of angels and with the church on earth and in heaven:

All: *Singing*   GROSSER GOTT, WIR LOBEN DICH
Holy God, we praise your name;
   Sovereign God, we come before you;
All on earth your scepter claim,
   all the heavenly hosts adore you,
and in awe we reverently
   seek the sacred mystery.

Words: Anon. German, c. 1774,
trans. Clarence Alphonsus Walwroth, 1853, alt.

Minister: Holy One, stay with us for this holy meal.
Bless us and these gifts we offer from the bounty of your creation:
Bread baked from many individual grains milled together into one flour
and wine fermented from many individual grapes crushed together
to be for us your body and blood.
Give us a sacramental seeing that our eyes may be opened
that we may know the risen Christ present here.

All: **We offer ourselves to you — heart and soul, mind and body,**
that you will use us as instruments of your welcoming love.

*The minister recites the words of institution. Intercessions may be offered, and all pray the
Lord's Prayer.*

Minister: The gifts of God for the people of God.
Come for everything is ready.

*The elements are distributed with appropriate words of administration. After all have
received, the service continues with the following:*

Leader 1: They said to each other,

Leaders 2 & 3:
"Were not our hearts burning within us
while he was talking to us on the road,
while he was opening the Scriptures to us?"

Leader 1: Then they told what had happened on the road,
and how he had been made known to them
in the breaking of the bread.   —Luke 24:32, 35

Minister: Our hearts burn with thanksgiving, O God,
for uniting us at this table with Christ crucified and risen.

All: **Now send us out to tell a waiting world what has happened to us
and how Christ has been made known to us in this sacred meal.
Open our eyes to meet the strangers who join us on our way,
to invite them to table again, and to recognize again
the One who comes as stranger to give us more than bread alone.
Amen.**

◆◆◆   6.1.10

The following liturgy for the Eucharist is crafted for the Fourth Sunday of Easter, commonly known as "Good Shepherd Sunday." This expression also includes the corresponding prayer of thanksgiving and sending rite. The initial petitions of the Eucharistic prayer may be prayed by two ministers, one saying the "Jesus" passages, and the other the "We" passages.

Minister: Lift up your hearts!

All: **We lift them up to the Lord!**

Minister: Jesus, Son of God, we lift our hearts in thankful remembrance
of your reconciling love, outpoured on the cross once and for all time.

All: **We praise you for your victory over the powers of evil and death,
assuring us that neither life nor death nor anything in all creation
can separate us from the love of God.**

Minister: Jesus, Good Shepherd, you laid down your own life
that others may have life and have it abundantly.

All: **We thank you for naming us the lambs of your own redeeming
and enfolding us in the flock of your shepherding care.**

Minister: Jesus, Bread of Life, you are the living bread
come down from heaven for the life of the world.

All: **We pray that you will break this bread for us,
that it may be your body broken to feed us
until we feast at last at the heavenly table.**

Minister: Jesus, True Vine, you are the life-giving source
apart from which the branches cannot flower by themselves,
yet, if they abide in you bear fruit abundantly.

All: **We pray that you will fill this cup for us,
that it may be your blood poured out for us,
and that, drinking of it, we shall never thirst again.**

Minister: Jesus, Light of the World, whoever follows you
will never walk in darkness but will have the light of life.

All: **We offer you ourselves, our souls and bodies, a living sacrifice,
dedicated to your service and united in a common ministry,
that all may come to believe you are the Christ
and, in believing, may have new life in your name.**

The minister may recite the words of institution while breaking the bread and pouring the cup. All may pray the Lord's Prayer.

A setting of the traditional Agnus Dei *or the following adaptation may be sung by a choir or the assembly. If the latter is used, it may be repeated as many times as may be deemed appropriate. The keyboard accompaniment may be found on page 212. It may be accompanied also with the steady beat of an Indian drum or muffled snare.*

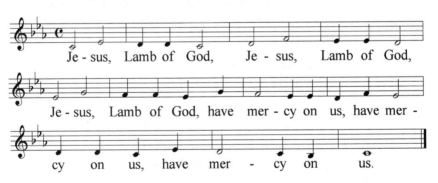

Je - sus, Lamb of God, Je - sus, Lamb of God,
Je - sus, Lamb of God, have mer - cy on us, have mer -
cy on us, have mer - cy on us.

Music copyright © 2004 F. Russell Mitman

After all have communed, the following prayer of thanksgiving may be prayed in unison.

All: **Jesus, Good Shepherd, who laid down your life for us all,
We thank you for feeding us with holy mysteries
that assure us you know us and we belong to you.
Keep us ever in the fold of your care,
and anoint us with your healing grace,
that we may continue to hear your voice,
and follow you in faith. Amen.**

Leader: Now may the God of peace,
who brought back from the dead our Lord Jesus,
the great shepherd of the sheep,
by the blood of the eternal covenant
make you complete in everything good
so that you may do God's will,
working among you that which is pleasing in God's sight,
through Jesus Christ, to whom be the glory forever and ever.

—Hebrews 13:20–21

All: **Amen.**

Leader: Go in peace to serve the Lord.

All: **Thanks be to God!**

◆◆◆ 6.1.11

The following order for the Eucharist on Pentecost is patterned after the scriptural account of the Pentecost event as recorded in the second chapter of Acts, juxtaposed with an altered version of Henry Hallam Tweedy's famous hymn and a doxological phrase from the ancient Latin hymn Veni Creator Spiritus. *The words "O Spirit of the Living God" may be sung to several tunes:* ST. MATTHEW, ELLACOMBE, NOEL, *or* FOREST GREEN. *The initial exhortation is creedal in nature, and it may serve as the setting for the placement of the elements on the altar table.*

Minister: Jesus has been raised by God,

All: **and of that all of us are witnesses.**

Minister: Exalted at the right hand of God,
Christ received the promise of the Holy Spirit.
and has poured out all that you now see and hear.
For the promise is for you, for your children,
and for all who are far off.

All: **Everyone whom the Lord our God calls.**   —Acts 2:32–33, 39, adapt.

Minister: Come, Holy Spirit, come, and prepare our hearts
as we set the table for this holy feast
with the gifts of your creation and the offerings of our lives.

All: **Amen.**

As the assembly's gifts are received, the congregation may sing a hymn such as Fred Kaan's "Let Us Talents and Tongues Employ," Robert Edwards's "God Whose Giving Knows No Ending," or "Like the Murmur of the Dove's Song" by Carl P. Daw, Jr.

Minister: We thank you, O God, for the gift of your Holy Spirit.

By the power of your creating Spirit
you brought the worlds into being,
and you breathe the breath of life into every living thing,
forming us in your image
and uniting all that is in a cosmic dependence.

From heaven you sent your baptizing Spirit
upon your own beloved Son amidst Jordan's water
and anointed him as the bearer of your salvation,
that all who are baptized into his life and death and resurrection
may share in the new life Christ offers the world.

With the rush of a mighty wind
your Spirit founded the church on Pentecost,
and by that same Spirit you continually shower upon us
a multitude of spiritual gifts, renewing and empowering your church
to continue Christ's work of preaching and teaching and healing.

All: *Singing*
**O Spirit of the Living God, O Light and Holy Fire,
Descend upon your church once more, our dreams and hopes inspire.
Fill us with love and joy and power, with righteousness and peace,
Till Christ shall dwell in human hearts and sin and sorrow cease.**
Words: Henry Hallam Tweedy, 1933, alt.

Minister: Holy Spirit, pass through our gathering at this table
to bless us and these gifts of bread and wine,
that the bread we break and the cup we bless
may be the communion of the body and blood of Christ.
Unite us with all who share this feast in heaven and on earth,
until we shall banquet at last with all the saints in glory.

All: **Amen.**

Minister: With your people of every age we offer this sacrifice of joyous thanksgiving.

All: **Praise to your eternal merit, Father, Son, and Holy Spirit.**

Unison: **Amen.**

The minister breaks the bread and pours the cup with words of institution. Then all pray the Lord's Prayer.

Minister: *Administering the bread*
The bread of heaven given for you.

Each person: Amen.

Minister: *Administering the cup*
The cup of salvation shed for you.

Each person: Amen.

After all have been served the service continues with the following thanksgiving:

Minister: Holy God, we rejoice that you have fed us at this table
with the spiritual food of the body and blood of Christ,
and have united us in communion
with your church on earth and in heaven.
Grant us the abiding presence of your Holy Spirit.
Enrich our faith.
Nourish us through the means of grace.
Strengthen our life together.
Confirm us in our ministry and mission.
And, with glad and generous hearts,
may we praise you and find favor with all people,
to the honor and glory of Jesus Christ.

All: **Amen.**

◆◆◆   6.1.12

In the following each of the four sentences in each section of the Eucharistic prayer may be prayed by one of four officiating ministers. The "from above" is a reference to Jesus' conversations with Nicodemus in John 3:1ff. The structure obviously is Trinitarian, and this liturgy may be used on Trinity Sunday when the story of Jesus and Nicodemus is appointed or on general occasions. The post-communion thanksgiving leads naturally into a sending act.

Minister: The Lord be with you.

All: **And also with you.**

Minister: Lift up your hearts!

All: **We lift them to the Lord!**

Minister: Let us give thanks to the Lord our God.

All: **It is right to give our thanks and praise.**

Singing:

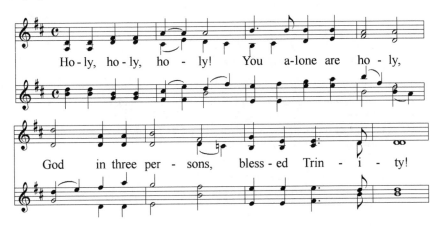

Ho-ly, ho-ly, ho - ly! You a-lone are ho - ly,

God in three per - sons, bless - ed Trin - i - ty!

Words: Reginald Heber, 1826, adapt.; Music: John Bacchus Dykes, 1861, adapt.

Minister: Out of a formless void you shaped the world and all living things
and continue to breathe into them the breath of life
and to declare all creation good.
From above you watch over the world,
seeking in fatherly caring and motherly nurturing to protect and discipline
your own beloved but often erring and straying children.
You continue to send us prophets and apostles
to remind us that all creation is your gift,
a precious planting in need of our vigilant tending.
In holy love you come to us, driving out our fears
and assuring us that we are not left to wallow in the sins
of our own devices and desires.

All: *Singing*
Holy, holy, holy! Merciful and mighty!
God in three persons, blessed Trinity!

Minister: In Jesus Christ you became flesh and continue to dwell among us
in reconciling grace and redeeming truth,
promising the whole world a new creation.
Through Jesus' life, death, resurrection, and ascension
you have revealed yourself to us, allowing us to glimpse who you are
in the midst of our own finiteness and humanness.
From above, in Christ you birth us anew into a wholehearted trust
and beckon us to press on toward the upward call of Christ
into his new realm of justice and witness.
In body and soul, in life and death,

our only comfort is that we belong not to ourselves
but to our faithful Savior, Jesus Christ.

All: *Singing*
Holy, holy, holy! Merciful and mighty!
God in three persons, blessed Trinity!

Minister: By the power of your Holy Spirit you create and renew your church,
binding in covenant faithful people of all ages, tongues, and races.
From above you shower a variety of the Spirit's gifts,
empowering and commissioning us for Jesus' ministry
of preaching, teaching, and healing.
Through your Spirit we are re-spirited
for lives of joyful service and grateful giving.
Therefore, with patriarchs and prophets, apostles and martyrs,
with all the saints on earth and in heaven
who have witnessed to your power,
with your holy church throughout all the world, we give you thanks.

All: *Singing*
Holy, holy, holy! Merciful and mighty!
God in three persons, blessed Trinity!

Minister: We offer you this bread and wine,
together with the offering of our thanksgiving and praise.
By your Holy Spirit sanctify us and these gifts,
that we may be nourished through these holy mysteries,
and be strengthened for your service in the name of Jesus Christ.

All: **Amen.**

The minister repeats the words of institution together with the manual acts of breaking the bread and pouring the cup. All pray the Lord's Prayer. After all have communed, the service continues:

Minister: For sacred mysteries more wondrous than our hearts can imagine
and our minds can discern,
For a holy presence more miraculous than our souls can fathom
and our spirits can comprehend,
For a blessed communion more embracing than our relationships
can encompass and our reasoning can allow,
For spiritual giftings more empowering than our faith can confess
and our wills can admit,
For an abundance of grace more amazing than hope can hope for
and love can love,

All: **Receive, O God, our joyful thanks and praise.**

| Leader: | May the Lord give strength to God's people. |
| | May the Lord bless the people with peace. |

—Psalm 29:11

| Leader: | "Then I heard the voice of the Lord saying, |
| | 'Whom shall I send, and who will go for us?'" |

| All: | *Shouting* |
| | **Here am I; send me!** |

—Isaiah 6:8

◆◆◆ 6.1.13

| Minister: | The grace of the Lord Jesus Christ, the love of God, |
| | and the communion of the Holy Spirit be with you. |

| All: | **And also with you.** |

| Minister: | Lift up your hearts! |

| All: | **We lift them to the Lord!** |

| Minister: | Let us give thanks to the Triune God. |

| All: | **It is right to give our thanks and praise.** |

Minister:	At your call creation was birthed out of chaos
	and by your breath the world and all living things came into being
	and continually are sustained.

| All: | **Receive, O God, our thanks and praise.** |

Minister:	At your call Moses led your people from slavery to freedom,
	and people of all ages, tongues, and races
	are brought from bondage to the day of promise.

| All: | **Receive, O God, our thanks and praise.** |

Minister:	At your call prophets and apostles recall people and nations
	from aimlessness and sin to the daylight of justice and righteousness,
	and you offer the world new ways to reconciliation and peace.

| All: | **Receive, O God, our thanks and praise.** |

| Minister: | In Christ you became flesh of our flesh and dwelt among humankind, |
| | calling the world continually to glimpse your glory. |

| All: | **Receive, O Christ, our thanks and praise.** |

Minister:	In Christ you suffered the humiliation of the cross
	and triumphed in his resurrection,
	calling all people from the tombs of death to the garden of new life.

| All: | **Receive, O Christ, our thanks and praise.** |

Minister: In Christ you call the world to repentance
and offer to all who turn to him the power to become children of God.

All: **Receive, O Christ, our thanks and praise.**

Minister: Through the Holy Spirit you call the church to faithful discipleship,
summoning men and women, youth and children,
to take up the cross and follow where Christ will lead.

All: **Receive, O Holy Spirit, our thanks and praise.**

Minister: Through the Holy Spirit you call ordinary people to mission and ministry,
empowering them with the gifts to preach, to teach, and to heal
in the name of Jesus.

All: **Receive, O Holy Spirit, our thanks and praise.**

Minister: Through the Holy Spirit you touch people with sacred signs and seals,
calling the world from a secular numbness into a holiness
that is heaven's gift.

All: **Receive, O Holy Spirit, our thanks and praise.**

Minister: With the church on earth in communion with all the saints,
we sing our thanks and praise, calling on your holy name:

All: *Singing*   NICAEA
Holy, holy, holy, Lord God Almighty!
All your works shall praise your name in earth and sky and sea;
Holy, holy, holy! merciful and mighty!
God in three Persons, blessed Trinity!

Words: Reginald Heber, 1827, adapt.

Minister: Bless us, holy God, at this table,
and bless these gifts of bread and wine that we offer you,
offerings from your creation to feed us with the means of grace.
Set them apart from their ordinary to a sacred and mystical use
that they may be to us the body and blood of Christ,
and that here we may eat and drink with Christ and all the saints
in glory everlasting. Amen.

All: **Christ has died, Christ is risen, and Christ will come again!**

The minister breaks the bread and pours the cup while reciting the words of institution. All pray the Lord's Prayer. After all have communed, the service continues with the following:

Minister: For feeding us with the spiritual food of the body and blood of Christ,
For nourishing us with those whom you have called into community,
For refreshing us with more than our minds can imagine
and our hearts can desire,

All: **Receive, O God, our thanks and praise.**

◆◆◆ 6.1.14

The following liturgy is particularly appropriate for the Pentecost season. It includes two elements from the Continental Reformed tradition. The initial versicle traces its origin to St. Cyprian, but it is translated and adapted here from the Palatinate Liturgy of 1563. The post-communion affirmation is an adaptation of the first question of the Heidelberg Catechism *completed in the same year. The unison metrical prayers before and after Communion are my attempts to preserve the concept that Eucharistic prayers began as table graces before and after the holy meal. The first one has familiar elements of an old German table grace. Both, as well as the final doxology, may be sung to* OLD HUNDREDTH *or another suitable long meter tune. The elements may be placed on the altar table during the initial versicle.*

Minister: As many individual grains are milled together into one flour
          and one loaf is baked,
          and as many individual grapes are pressed together
          and flow into one wine,

All: **So shall we be incorporated together in love,
      for the sake of Christ our Savior,
      who loves us and calls us to show forth his love in word and deed.**

Minister: We remember, O God, that from the beginning
          you have called your people together into the household of faith
          and have bound us together
          with the signs and seals of your everlasting covenant.

          We rejoice that in Jesus Christ, and through the one offering of himself,
          we who are buried and raised with him in baptism
          are incorporated into his body and made living members of his church.

          We give thanks that you have called us to be at one with all the saints
          who in every place call on his name
          and with whom we too are united in one communion.

          By the blessing of your Holy Spirit sanctify us and this bread and wine,
          that we may be nourished in the body through these holy mysteries,
          and strengthened for service in the name of Jesus Christ.

All: *Singing*
      **Come, Jesus, Lord, and be our guest
      To share with us communion blest;
      And with this bread and wine impart
      Your grace to every waiting heart.**

The minister repeats the words of institution in the customary manner, breaking the bread and pouring the cup appropriately. All pray the Lord's Prayer, and the Communion may be distributed with appropriate words of administration. After all have received the service continues with the following.

Minister: Let us give thanks.

All: *Singing*
We thank you, Lord, for holy food:
Our Christ's own body, his own blood,
The Bread of Life, the Branches' Vine,
To feed and nourish humankind.

Minister: What is your only comfort in life and in death?

All: That I belong — body and soul, in life and death —
not to myself but to my faithful Savior, Jesus Christ,
who at the cost of his own blood has fully paid for my sins.
By his Holy Spirit he assures me of eternal life
and makes me wholeheartedly willing and ready
from now on to live for him.

Question 1, *Heidelberg Catechism,* adapt.

All: *Singing*
Praise God from whom all blessings flow. . . .

◆◆◆ 6.1.15

*In the following the communion elements may be presented during the initial hymn stanzas.
In most hymnals these words of Horatius Bonar are set to* MORECAMBE *and sometimes to
the Benedictine plainsong* ADORO TE DEVOTE. *An alternative tune, as indicated here is*
ELLERS. *This expression is shaped by the Synoptic story of Jesus feeding the five thousand
and the corresponding imagery in the Old Testament accounts of God's gift of manna in the
wilderness.*

Minister: This is the joyful feast of the people of God!
Come from the east and the west and from the north and the south,
and gather around the Lord's table.

All: *Singing*   ELLERS
Here, O our Lord, we see you face to face;
here would we touch and handle things unseen,
here grasp with firmer hand eternal grace,
and all our weariness upon you lean.

Here would we feed upon the bread of God,
Here drink with you the royal wine of heaven;
Here would we lay aside each earthly load,
Here taste afresh the calm of sin forgiven.

Minister: We come to your table, O Lord, prepared to feast with only a scanty fare.
We come with so little —
so little devotion, so little commitment, so little love.

Our hunger is so great, and the world's needs are so many.
The storehouses where we go to buy bread seem empty,
and what are these few gifts we bring to a world so starved?
Yet, as manna showered miraculously from heaven on hungry wanderers
and you fed crowds with but five loaves and two fish,
we ask you to take these meager gifts we offer you,
and we pray you to bless them, break them,
and give them again to us sacramentally,
that at table with all who hunger we may find ourselves mysteriously filled
and shall discover, left over, baskets brimming to feed a waiting world.

All: *Singing*   ELLERS
This is the hour of banquet and of song;
This is the heavenly table for us spread;
Here let us feast and, feasting, still prolong
The sacrament of living wine and bread.

The minister shall repeat the words of institution while breaking the bread and pouring the cup. Intercession may be included, and all pray the Lord's Prayer. After all have communed, the service continues with the following thanksgiving.

Minister: For the bread that, more than bread alone,
nourishes our bodies to be your body throughout the earth
and feeds our souls with food for eternal life,

All: **Receive our thanks, O Christ!**

Minister: For the wine that, poured out in your self-sacrifice for us,
revives our souls and refreshes our bodies for life together in your church,

All: **Receive our thanks, O Christ!**

Minister: Now empower us to share the words and deeds of your wondrous grace
with all who hunger for justice and righteousness,
and thirst for healing and wholeness.

All: **Amen.**

All: *Singing*   ELLERS
Too soon we rise; the symbols disappear.
The feast, though not the love, is past and gone;
The bread and wine remove, but you are here,
Nearer than ever, still our shield and sun.

Feast after feast thus comes and passes by,
Yet, passing, points to that glad feast above,
Giving sweet foretaste of the festal joy,
The Lamb's great bridal feast of bliss and love.

Words: Horatius Bonar, 1855, alt.

◆◆◆ 6.1.16

The following Eucharistic prayer is shaped by Psalm 96:7–13. It may be used on those occasions when this Psalm is appointed or on other occasions celebrating God's creation. It begins with an acclamation that may begin immediately after the sermon or as a prelude to the offering. The Eucharistic prayer is prefaced with the singing of Henry M. Butler's creative setting of the ancient Sursum Corda *("Lift up your hearts"), which may be used as the offertory response. Generally these words are set to* WOODLANDS *although* ELLERS *and* EVENTIDE *are more familiar tunes to most congregations.*

Although Calvin abandoned the use of most other elements of the mass in his 1542 liturgy, he retained the Sursum Corda *because it expressed the sense that the Eucharistic action takes place in heaven, where Christ is and to whom believers lift their hearts in faith. Therefore, "Lord" here and in the other liturgies that have included the* Sursum Corda *intentionally is interpreted Christologically.*

Leader: Ascribe to the Lord, O families of the peoples,
ascribe to the Lord glory and strength!

All: Ascribe to the Lord the glory due God's name!

Leader: Bring an offering, and come into the courts of the Lord!

All: Worship the Lord in holy splendor!   —Psalm 96:7–9a, adapt.

The offering is received. A musical setting of Psalm 96 may be sung by a choir or by the assembly.

Response: Singing   WOODLANDS
"Lift up your hearts!" We lift them, Lord, to you,
for it is always rightful so to do.
"Lift up your hearts!" e'en so, with one accord,
we lift them up, we lift them to the Lord.

Above the level of the former years,
the mire of sin, the weight of guilty fears,
the mist of doubt, the blight of love's decay,
O Lord of light, lift all our hearts today!

Lift every gift that you yourself have given.
Low lies the best till lifted up to heaven.
Low lie the bounding heart, the teeming brain,
till sent from God, they mount to God again.

Then as the trumpet call, in after years,
"Lift up you hearts!" rings pealing in our ears,
still shall those hearts respond, with full accord,
"We lift them up, we lift them to the Lord."

Words: Henry M. Butler, 1881, alt.

Leader: Say among the nations, "The Lord reigns!"

All: **The world is firmly established, it shall never be moved.**
The Lord will judge the peoples with equity.

Leader: Let the heavens be glad, and let the earth rejoice;
Let the sea roar, and all that fills it;
let the field rejoice, and everything in it!

All: **Then shall all the trees of the forest sing for joy before the Lord,**
The Lord will judge the world with righteousness,
and the peoples with truth.   —Psalm 96:10–13, adapt.

Minister: Let us give thanks to the Lord our God.

All: **It is right to give our thanks and praise.**

Minister: We thank you, O God, that you have marked your creation
with the signs and seasons of your splendor.
You remind us that you alone are the image in which we are created
and that all others are the idols of our own making.
You alone are God, and all other allegiances
are gods of our own fashioning.
In Christ, the Word made flesh, you have destroyed the powers of sin
and have smashed the idols that would demand any divided devotion.
In him alone is life, and his life is the life of all people.
To all who receive him he gives power to become your children.
Through your Holy Spirit you empower the ones you call out
to shape a new community that is in the world yet not of it
and that is able to discern, in a culture of competing loyalties,
what belongs alone to you and to your realm.
In concert with the voices of those who have gone before us
and the choirs of angels that surround you in heaven,
we join in a new song to sing your praise:

All: *Singing*   GROSSER GOTT, WIR LOBEN DICH
Holy God, we praise your name; Lord of all, we bow before you.
All on earth your scepter claim, all in heaven above adore you.
Infinite your vast domain, everlasting is your reign!

Another stanza may be added:

Holy Father, Holy Son, Holy Spirit: Three we name you.
While in essence only One, Undivided God we claim you.
And, adoring, bend the knee while we own the mystery.

Minister: You are holy, O God of majesty,
and blessed is Jesus Christ, your Son, our Lord.
In remembrance of all your mighty and merciful acts,

we ask you to take this bread and wine we offer you
as gifts we return from your creation.
Accept this our sacrifice of thanksgiving and praise
as a living and holy offering of ourselves,
that we may become instruments of your word
to all seeking to turn away from idols to serve the living God.

Minister: Great is the mystery of faith.

All: **Christ has died, Christ is risen, Christ will come again.**

The minister repeats the words of institution together with the manual acts of breaking the bread and pouring the cup. Intercessions may be included. All pray the Lord's Prayer. After all have communed the service continues:

Minister: At this table, holy God, you have touched us
with things more wondrous than we can fathom.
You have given us bread which is more than bread,
and a cup that brims with more than we can drink.
Now send us into a world cluttered with the idols of human making
to witness to the truth that you, and you alone,
have sovereign power over peoples and nations,
and that your kingdom will come, your will shall be done
on earth as it is in heaven.

All: **Amen.**

◆◆◆ 6.1.17

In the following the anamnesis *portion of the Eucharistic prayer is patterned after the United Church of Christ Statement of Faith in the Form of a Doxology. The keyboard accompaniment may be found on page 213.*

Minister: Lift up your hearts!

All: **We lift them up to the Lord!**

Minister: Let us give thanks to God.

All: **It is right to give God thanks and praise.**

Minister: We give thanks to you, O God,
and with the church in every place and setting
we join our hearts to praise you, Eternal Spirit,
God of our Savior Jesus Christ
and our God, and to your deeds we testify:

All: **You call the worlds into being, create persons in your own image,
and set before each one the ways of life and death.**

You seek in holy love to save all people from aimlessness and sin.
You judge people and nations by your righteous will
   declared through prophets and apostles.
In Jesus Christ, the man of Nazareth,
   our crucified and risen Savior,
   you have come to us and shared our common lot,
   conquering sin and death and reconciling the world to yourself.
You bestow upon us your Holy Spirit,
   creating and renewing the church of Jesus Christ,
   binding in covenant faithful people
   of all ages, tongues, and races.
You call us into your church
   to accept the cost and joy of discipleship,
   to be your servants in the service of others,
   to proclaim the Gospel to all the world
   and resist the powers of evil,
   to share in Christ's baptism and eat at his table,
   to join him in his passion and victory.
You promise to all who trust you
   forgiveness of sins and fullness of grace,
   courage in the struggle for justice and peace,
   your presence in trial and rejoicing,
   and eternal life in your realm which has no end.

Singing:

Bless-ing and hon-or, glo-ry and power be un-to you! A - men.

Words: United Church of Christ Statement of Faith in the Form of a Doxology, 1981;
Music: copyright © 2004 F. Russell Mitman.

Minister: From the bounty of your abundant creation
     we offer you these simple gifts of bread and wine.
   We ask you to bless them and to bless us
     as we receive them at this table,
     that through the power of your Holy Spirit
     they may become for us the body and blood
     of our Savior Jesus Christ.

All: **Join us with his church in heaven and on earth**
              until at last we feast face to face with all the saints
              in the glorious communion of your heavenly realm.

Minister: Great is the mystery of faith.

All: **Christ has died, Christ is risen, Christ will come again!**

The minister breaks the bread and pours the cup while repeating the words of institution. All pray the Lord's Prayer. After all have communed the service continues:

Minister: Give thanks to the Lord who is good,

All: **God's steadfast love endures forever!**   —Psalm 118:29, alt.

Minister: Good and generous God,
              we give you thanks for giving us all that is necessary for life,
              and for nourishing us through Word and Sacrament with holy things
              that unite us with Christ and with one another.

All: **Your steadfast love endures forever.**

Minister: Through your Holy Spirit you empower the church
              to continue Christ's mission of preaching, teaching, and healing,
              that far and near people of all ages, tongues, and races
              may be touched with your transforming grace.

All: **Your steadfast love endures forever.**

Minister: Now send us from this place to meet Christ in other places
              where he will beckon us to follow him, inviting us and many
              to accept the cost and joy of discipleship
              in a world crying for justice, reconciliation, and peace.

All: *singing*
              Blessing and honor, glory and power, be unto you! Amen.

◆◆◆ 6.1.18

The following liturgy for a celebration of the unity of the church is especially appropriate for World Communion Sunday or for use during the Week of Prayer for Christian Unity. John Oxenham's famous hymn "In Christ There Is No East or West" serves as the framework. The hymn is set to a number of tunes and appears in some recent inclusive language adaptations. I shall leave it to the leader to decide which setting of the words and which tune is appropriate, and I shall merely indicate which stanza is to be sung. No instrumental introduction is necessary.

Minister: Beloved, this is the joyful feast of the people of God.
              Come from the east and from the west
              and from the north and from the south,
              and gather around the Lord's table.

All: Behold how good and pleasant it is
            when sisters and brothers dwell in unity!

—Adapted by permission of the publisher from
Service of Word and Sacrament I, © 1966 United Church Press

Sing stanza 1.

Minister: Lift up your hearts!

All: We give thanks, O God, for calling us to this table
            and joining us here with your people of all ages, tongues, and races
            throughout the whole wide earth.
            We remember your saving love,
            calling all people from bondage to freedom
            and reconciling the whole world to yourself through Jesus Christ.
            We rejoice in the presence of your Holy Spirit,
            filling the earth with the power that unites and brings peace.

            Bless us at this table and those at every table in every place.
            Feed us with the one bread, and make us drink of one cup,
            that we may be united with Christ and sent forth
            to offer ourselves as instruments of reconciliation and peace.

Sing stanza 2.

The minister repeats the words of institution. All pray the Lord's Prayer, and the minister may use any appropriate words of administration. Alternate words during the distribution for this or for any other services are as follows:

    Bread—*John 6:35, 47–51, 10:14–16, 13:34–35, 14:27;*

    Cup—*John 15:1–11 or John 15:1–17*

After Communion, sing verses 3 and 4. A visible sign of unity may be given, such as a handshake, embrace, or joining of hands. If the congregation is gathered around the table, it is appropriate to join hands during a benediction.

◆◆◆   6.1.19

The following is designed for use on All Saints' Day or All Saints' Sunday. It may be prefaced with a table-setting reading of Isaiah 25:6–9 either before the offering is received or following the offering as a prelude to this Eucharistic prayer. The keyboard accompaniment for the Sanctus *may be found on page 214. Bongo drums or other percussion instruments will enhance the festive style of this setting. It should not be sung slowly. It may be repeated several times. The final hymn stanzas may be sung to* SINE NOMINE *or* ENGELBERG.

Minister: Lift up your hearts!

All: We lift them to the God of our salvation!

Minister: In Jesus Christ, O God, you are calling us from death into life:
calling us from the tombs of our despair
  into the freedom of your hope,
calling us from the darkness of our fears
  into the light of your love,
calling us from the emptiness of our relationships
  into the fullness of your presence,
calling us from the everydayness of our world
  into the splendor of your realm.

All: **Thanks be to God who gives us the victory
through our Lord Jesus Christ.**

Minister: *Breaking the bread*
We remember that on the night before his death,
Jesus took bread and blessed, and broke it,
and gave it to the disciples and said,
"Take, eat, this is my body."

Pouring the cup
And he took a cup, and when he had given thanks,
he gave it to them, saying,
"Drink of it, all of you, for this is my blood of the new covenant
which is poured out for many for the forgiveness of sins.
I tell you I shall not drink again of this fruit of the vine
until that day when I drink it anew with you in my Father's kingdom."

All: **Amen. Come, Lord Jesus!**

Minister: We remember also that on the day of resurrection,
when Jesus was at table with two of the disciples,
he took the bread, blessed and broke it and gave it to them;
and their eyes were opened, and they recognized him.

All: **Amen. Come, Lord Jesus!**

Minister: In our remembering, unite us sacramentally in Christ's resurrected life,
that we may be nourished through these holy mysteries until,
with the redeemed of all ages who have lived and died in Christ,
we may feast at last in the full communion of all the saints.

All: **Amen. Come, Lord Jesus!**

Minister: In thanksgiving we hold sacred those faithful women and men who have
followed Jesus' calling and touched our lives with their witness
and whom we now name before you: *name(s)*
Surrounded at this table by your faithful ones in heaven and on earth,
we join our voices with them to sing your praise:

All: *Singing, lively,*

Ho - ly, ho - ly, ho - ly Lord, God of pow - er and might. hea - ven and earth are full of your glo - ry. Ho - san - na in the high - est. - Bles - sed the one who comes in the name of the Lord. Ho - san - na in the high - est.

Music copyright © 2001 F. Russell Mitman

Minister: Together with these gifts of bread and wine, O God,
we offer ourselves in joyful obedience
to summon all who still are wrapped in the death-bands of defeat
into the resurrection-life of Christ's liberating promise:
"I will come again and will take you to myself,
so that where I am, there you may be also."

All: **Amen!**
Thanks be to God who gives us the victory
through our Lord Jesus Christ!

Intercessions may be offered, and all pray the Lord's Prayer.

Minister: Come, for all things are ready!

After all have communed, the service continues:

Minister: Behold, the dwelling of God is with mortals
God will dwell with them as their God;
they will be God's peoples, and God will be with them;
God will wipe every tear from their eyes.
Death will be no more;
mourning and crying and pain will be no more,
for the former things have passed away.

All: *Singing*
         For all the saints who from their labors rest,
         who to the world their steadfast faith confessed,
         Your name, O Jesus, be forever blessed. Alleluia! Alleluia!

         You were their rock, their refuge and their might;
         You, Lord, their captain in the well-fought fight;
         You, in the darkness drear, their one true light. Alleluia! Alleluia!

         Ringed by this cloud of witnesses divine,
         we feebly struggle, they in glory shine;
         yet in your love our faithful lives entwine. Alleluia! Alleluia!

                                          Words: William Walsham How, 1864, alt.

Chapter Seven

Sending

Whatever occurs following the Eucharist is very brief. The pilgrimage that led us to this hour of interaction with God and one another carries us again out the doors and challenges us to follow a Christ who is always ahead of his people. Just as worship has it moments of remembering the past and its present encounters, so also it has its future orientation. The theological adjective is "eschatological." From the human perspective it is the awareness of a certain unfinishedness about the Sunday hour. We feel that we cannot be satisfied with a "good-bye" that has no qualifying "until" about it — until Christ meets us again, and until we meet each other again, and that meeting most often will be somewhere outside the sanctuary, in the world, where Christ already is, beckoning the assembly to follow. The divine-human interaction hopes for reunion and ultimate union at some point that is "not-yet."

Therefore, any charge and/or words of benediction are an interim blessing of the pilgrims for the pilgrimage. The service is over, yes, but the service continues in another form. The procession that began at the font is still moving toward the future. We are not a mighty army of Christian soldiers marching as to war but a band of exiles whose homeland and destiny lies in the promises and providence of God: Hence my same caution about recessionals as with processionals — they need to acknowledge that our being has its origins and destiny beyond the rhythm of our own feet. Sometimes the recessional of choir and/or clergy may be joined in by the whole congregation without any break. Conversely, as may be quite appropriate on Palm Sunday when palms are sometimes distributed, the congregation may lead the recessional, being followed by choir and clergy. Even in buildings in which the choir is located in a gallery, there are occasions for recessionals to symbolize quite dramatically the movement of people of God on and out into the world.

The emphasis ought to be upon movement out into the world and away from the gathering place. It is just the opposite of the movement from the world and into the holy place with which the service began. Hence, I

185

believe that sending acts ought to have their origin in the chancel and move to the rear of the church building. Blessings and choral responses from the rear, although aesthetically pleasing, interrupt the movement. However, if the font is located at the rear of the sanctuary, the charge and blessing may be a beckoning by the leader for the assembly to follow their baptismal commission for service into the world. Sitting down following the hymn for quiet meditation accompanied by organ chimes also is a disjunction. Calvin was quite right: the true offering of the Christian takes place after the service is over, and out in the world where our neighbors' needs call forth our service. Those needs are urgent, and nothing ought to detain us from getting on with that service.

EXHORTATIONS, BENEDICTIONS, AND OTHER RESOURCES _____

◆◆◆   7.1.1

Leader: Now may God make you increase and abound in love for one another
          and for all people, strengthening your hearts in holiness
          that you may be blameless before our God
          at the coming of our Lord Jesus.   —1 Thessalonians 3:11–13, adapt.

This may be followed by the singing of "Come, O Long-expected Jesus."

◆◆◆   7.1.2

The following may be used at a candlelight service.

Leader: Let your light shine before all people,
          so that they may see your good works
          and give glory to your Father who is in heaven.   —Matthew 5:16, adapt.

All may stand and raise candles high.

All: *Singing*
          Joy to the world, the Lord is come....

◆◆◆   7.1.3

Leader: Lord, now let your servant go in peace, according to your word.

All: **My eyes have seen your salvation**
          which you have prepared in the presence of all peoples,

Leader: A light for revelation to all nations,

All: **and for glory to your people Israel.**   —Luke 2:29–32, adapt.

◆◆◆ 7.1.4

Leader: Now may the God of peace give you peace at all times and in all ways.
         The Lord be with you all.   —2 Thessalonians 3:16, adapt.

All: **And also with you.**

All: *Singing or speaking*
         Amen.

The service may conclude with the exchange of peace.

◆◆◆ 7.1.5

*If the following is used on Easter, the final Alleluia may be replaced with the triple Alleluia
from the refrain of Cyril Atlington's hymn "Good Christian Men [Friends], Rejoice and
Sing," as set to the tune* GELOBT SEI GOTT *by Melchior Vulpius. It is appropriate to continue
singing additional verses as a closing hymn. Other suggestions are "The Day of Resurrection"
and "Thine Is the Glory." This blessing may be used throughout Eastertide as well. The words
of Jesus are adapted from John 14:27; 15:5, 9, 11.*

Leader: Go forth into the world with Christ's promise and blessing:
         "Peace I leave with you, peace such as the world cannot give.
         Let not your hearts be troubled, neither let them be afraid.
         I am the vine, and you are the branches;
         abide in my love that my joy may be in you, and your joy complete."
                                          —John 14:27; 15:5, 9, 11, adapt.

All: Praise and thanks to you, O Christ. Alleluia!

◆◆◆ 7.1.6

*In the following one person may speak the charge and another the blessing, or the leader may
speak both.*

Leader 1: Forgetting what lies behind
           and straining forward to what lies ahead,
           let us press on toward the goal for the prize
           of the heavenly call of God in Christ Jesus.

Leader 2: The grace of our Lord Jesus Christ be with you all.
                                          —Philippians 3:13–14; 4:23, adapt.

All:

A - men, A - men.

◆◆◆ 7.1.7

Isaac Watts paraphrased Psalm 72 Christologically in his great hymn "Jesus Shall Reign."
Here, prefaced by the glorious acclaim from Revelation 11:15, the psalm and the hymn are
set for use as a recessional. Since the blessing is announced both by the words of the psalm and
the text of the hymn, no additional benediction is necessary. In light of Watts's intention,
the "he" and "him" in the Psalm verses are interpreted Christologically to refer to the risen
Christ who now is the "King" referred to in the enthronement Psalm.

*   This hymn, when sung to* DUKE STREET, *is so familiar that no musical introduction other*
than a pedal note to establish pitch is necessary. An interlude with modulation to a higher
key may precede the last verse. A choral or instrumental descant may accompany the last
verse. On the last word, "Amen," sopranos may sing a fourth higher on "A----" and an octave
higher on "men." Tacking on an additional "amen" would be redundant.

Leader: The kingdom of this world has become the Kingdom of our Lord,
          and of his Christ.

All: **And he will reign forever and ever!**   —Revelation 11:15, alt.

All: *Singing*   DUKE STREET
          Jesus shall reign where're the sun
          **   does its successive journeys run,**
          His kingdom stretch from shore to shore,
          **   till moons shall wax and wane no more.**

Leader: May his name endure forever,
          his fame continue as long as the sun.

All: **May all nations be blessed in him.**   —Psalm 72:17

All: *Singing*
          People and realms of every tongue
          **   dwell on his love with sweetest song,**
          And infant voices shall proclaim
          **   the early blessings on his name.**

Leader: May he judge your people with righteousness,
            and your poor with justice.
        May the mountains yield prosperity for the people
            and the hills in righteousness.   —Psalm 72:2–4

All: *Singing*
Blessings abound where'er he reigns:
    the pris'ners leap to lose their chains,
The weary find eternal rest,
    and all who suffer want are blessed.

Leader: Blessed be the Lord, the God of Israel,
        who alone does wondrous things,

All: **Blessed be God's glorious name forever,**
may God's glory fill the earth!   —Psalm 72:18–19, alt.

All: *Singing*
Let ev'ry creature rise and bring
    honors peculiar to our King.
Angels descend with songs again,
    and earth repeat the loud Amen!

                  Hymn stanzas: Isaac Watts, 1719, alt.

◆◆◆   7.1.8

The blessing in the following is modeled on Christ's post-resurrection assurance recorded at the end of Matthew's Gospel. It is joined with adaptations of a similar commission in the appendix to Mark's Gospel and of the sending out of the seventy in the Gospel of Luke. A hymn of commission, such as "O Zion Haste, Your Mission High Fulfilling," may follow immediately.

Leader: Go into all the world and proclaim the good news to every creature,
        spread the saving word that God is near with wholeness and peace,
        and announce to every one Christ's eternal blessing and promise:
        "Lo, I am with you always, even to the end of time."

◆◆◆   7.1.9

Minister: May God fully satisfy every need of yours
        out of God's glorious riches in Jesus Christ.

All: **To our God be glory forever and ever!**

Leader: The grace of our Lord Jesus Christ be with you.

All: *Singing or speaking*
Amen!   —Philippians 4:19–20, 23, adapt.

◆◆◆   7.1.10

Minister: Grow in the grace and knowledge of our Lord and Savior Jesus Christ.

All: **To Christ be glory both now and for all eternity!**   —2 Peter 3:18, alt.

◆◆◆   7.1.11

All: *Singing*   CHRISTUS DER IS MEIN LEBEN
           Abide with us, our Savior, sustain us by your word,
           that we may now and ever, find peace in you, O Lord.

           Abide with us, our Savior, O light of endless Light;
           Bestow on us your blessing, and save us by your might.
                                                    Words: Joshua Stegmann, 1627 alt.

◆◆◆   7.1.12

The following also may be spoken by one person.

Leader 1: Rejoice in the Lord always; again I will say, Rejoice!
           Let your gentleness be known to everyone. The Lord is near.
           Do not worry about anything,
           but in everything by prayer and supplication with thanksgiving
           let your requests be made known to God.

Leader 2: And the peace of God which surpasses all understanding
           will guard your hearts and your minds in Christ Jesus. —Philippians 4:4–7

All: *Singing*   MARION
           Praise God who reigns on high,
           the Lord whom we adore,
           the Triune God who rules all worlds
           now and forevermore.
           Rejoice, rejoice, rejoice, give thanks and sing!
                                                    Words: Edward H. Plumptre, 1865, alt.

◆◆◆   7.1.13

The following is adapted from 1 Thessalonians 5:12–23. The charge and benediction may be spoken by two persons, respectively. During the exchange of peace the Israeli round "Shalom" may be sung, thereby concluding the service. Or, after sufficient time has been given for the exchange of peace, all may sing a hymn, such as "Love Divine All Loves Excelling" or the folk hymn "Peace I leave with You, My Friends."

Leader 1: We appeal to you, brothers and sisters, be at peace among yourselves.
           Encourage the fainthearted, help the weak, be patient with everyone.

Do not repay evil for evil, but hold fast to what is good.
Rejoice always, pray without ceasing, give thanks in all circumstances,
for this is the will of God in Christ Jesus for you.

Leader 2: May the God of peace sanctify you fully,
and may your spirit and soul and body be kept sound and blameless
at the coming of our Lord Jesus Christ.   —1 Thessalonians 5:12–23, adapt.

Leader 1: Let us give each other a sign of peace.

◆◆◆   7.1.14

The following may be spoken by three persons, respectively.

1. May the Lord bless you and take care of you;

2. May the Lord be kind and gracious to you;

3. May the Lord look on you with favor and give you peace.

—Numbers 6:24–26, TEV

These same three persons may also lead three groups of people (e.g., choir, the left side of the congregation, and the right side) in the singing of the following doxology as a round to TALLIS CANON *a cappella. Some may wish to substitute "Creator, Christ, and Holy Ghost" in the last line.*

Praise God from whom all blessings flow,
  Praise God, all creatures here below,
    Praise God, above, you heavenly host,
      Praise Father, Son, and Holy Ghost.

◆◆◆   7.1.15

Minister: May our Lord Jesus Christ and God our Father, who loves us
and through grace gives us eternal comfort and good hope,
comfort your hearts and strengthen them in every good work and word.
—2 Thessalonians 2:16, adapt.

◆◆◆   7.1.16

The following benediction and congregational response is designed to be sung. No additional words of benediction are necessary. It may be sung to any of the following tunes: RATHBUN, STUTTGART, CHARLESTOWN, *or* CROSS OF JESUS.

Solo or Choir:
      May the grace of Christ our Savior,
      the Creator's boundless love,
      and the Holy Spirit's favor
      rest upon us from above.

All: Thus may we abide in union
with each other and the Lord,
and possess, in sweet communion,
joys which earth cannot afford.

Words: John Newton, 1779, alt.

◆◆◆   7.1.17

Leader: The grace of Jesus Christ, the love of God,
and the sharing in the Holy Spirit be with you all.

—2 Corinthians 13:14

The assembly may share expressions of peace.

Leader: Go in peace to serve the Lord.

All: **Thanks be to God!**

◆◆◆   7.1.18

The following may be spoken by two leaders.

Leader: The peace of God which surpasses all understanding
keep your hearts and minds in Christ Jesus.   —Philippians 4:7, alt.

*The following may be added, and the leader and congregation may make the sign of the cross
as the words are spoken.*

Leader: The blessing of God Almighty:
Father, Son, and Holy Spirit,
be among you and remain with you always.

◆◆◆   7.1.19

In most hymnals, "Lord, Dismiss Us with Your Blessing" is set to SICILIAN MARINERS; *however, it also takes on new dimensions when sung to other tunes such as* LAUDA ANIMA, REGENT SQUARE, *and* WESTMINSTER ABBEY.

Leader: Now to the One who can keep you from falling
and to make you stand rejoicing in the presence of glory,

All: **To the only God our Savior, through Jesus Christ,
be glory, majesty, power, and authority,
before all time, now, and forevermore. Amen.**

—Jude 1:24–25, adapt.

All: *Singing*
         Lord, dismiss us with your blessing;
            fill our hearts with joy and peace;
         Let us each, your love possessing,
            triumph in redeeming grace:
         Oh, refresh us, oh, refresh us,
            traveling through this wilderness.

         Thanks we give and adoration
            for your Gospel's joyful sound;
         May the fruits of your salvation
            in our hearts and lives abound:
         Ever faithful, ever faithful
            to the truth may we be found.

Words: Attr. John Fawcett, 1773, alt.

 **7.1.20**

Although the following exhortation and blessing are designed to be spoken by two persons, one person may speak both.

Leader 1: And now, brothers and sisters, whatever is true,
           whatever is honorable, whatever is just, whatever is pure,
           whatever is pleasing, whatever is commendable,
           if there is any excellence and if there is anything worthy of praise,
           think about these things.

Leader 2: And may the God of peace be with you.   —Philippians 4:8–9, adapt.

♦♦♦   **7.1.21**

Leader: This service is over,

All: **but our service will never end!**

Chapter Eight

The Bulletins of Common Prayer

In 1884 a Chicago businessman by the name of A. B. Dick invented a duplicating process that has had more profound influence on worship and liturgics than perhaps any other invention. Nearly four hundred years earlier Johann Gutenberg's movable type had made a book of common prayer possible; A. B. Dick's mimeograph freed common prayer from the book. Despite the noble efforts of denominations to produce updated worship books and hymnals, usually by the time they are written, edited, published, bought by local churches, and placed in the pews, they have already passed into obsolescence. The mimeograph, however, allowed for the creation of a prayer book each week in the form of the Sunday bulletins. Struggling feverishly against the deadline of the service time, ministers got to handing Sunday's bulletins to the ushers fresh from the "holy roller" in the church office.

Since the publication of the first edition of this book nearly twenty years ago, another revolution has occurred that has taken what A. B. Dick's mimeograph first made possible to another level of sophistication, efficiency, and even economy, thereby opening up new ways of creating tools for the enactment of liturgy. Desktop publishing, which was ushered in by personal computers, coupled with copiers, made A. B. Dick's invention itself obsolete and even, perhaps, the part-time church secretary whose primary reason for being was to type the church bulletin unnecessary as well. This edition of this book includes a CD-ROM with all the resources downloadable at the click of a mouse button, and the worship leader, through the marvels of electronics, becomes the crafter of the media that will be the bearers of the liturgy's message. Computers and copiers are pieces of standard equipment that enable the resources of this book and its accompanying CD-ROM to become expressions of common worship.

During the past decades the entertainment culture has lured some churches into installing projection TV monitors and digital matrix screens into sanctuaries as replacements for printed bulletins and hymn books with the rationale that these free worshipers' hands for clapping and other liturgical gestures. Indeed, such devices do provide for some freedom of movement and do allow for image projection throughout the liturgy. However, they are large enough only for imaging of sing-along praise choruses or short prayers, and the impression is given that liturgy is a collection of individual, static acts. No monitor, however large the matrix, can capture the full range of the intrinsic flow of the liturgical action that can be included in a multipage printed bulletin.

Sunday bulletins have become the generally accepted prayer books of American Protestantism. Even Roman Catholics have adapted them in the form of disposable seasonal missals. Both Lutherans, who like to speak of "the" liturgy with its indigenous musical expressions, and Anglicans, who revere the Book of Common Prayer, find it necessary to publish bulletins as directories to indicate which setting or options will be used. Even though most denominations have some official versions of the liturgies for the sacraments and rites included in hymnals or in separate prayer books, the popular prayer books are the Sunday bulletins. A lot of people, I have discovered, collect bulletins; only clergy types and libraries collect prayer books. The more realistic picture of the worship life of most congregations is found not in what is printed in the front or back of the hymnals, nor in what is found in the prayer books in the pews, but in what is found in the ring binders church secretaries use to file copies of each Sunday's bulletin. Every pastor and worship committee can learn a great deal by studying seriously their bulletin anthologies. Those who complain that "everything's the same here week after week" will discover that really there have been changes, be they ever so slight. Conversely, those who complain that "nothing's the same here from one week to the next" will find an underlying pattern and structure that has about it a changeless quality affected not even by the call or appointment of a new pastor.

This means that even in churches that adhere to a denominational liturgy, there is a certain local uniqueness. No two churches are exactly alike in their liturgical expressions. Ever since Dick's invention made its way into church offices, and increasingly as denominational liturgies provide for even more alternative expressions, worship has been and will continue to be shaped according to congregationally determined patterns. The mimeograph once and for all freed parishes from denominational umbilical cords and placed far more responsibility for the integrity of the worship life of the church in the hands of local congregations — and especially today in the computerized word processors of parish ministers. That is the reason Sunday bulletins are so important, far more important than we sometimes suspect. What we do or do not do with Sunday bulletins has a profound effect on what happens worship-wise in each congregation, far more effect many times than the publication of a new hymnal or prayer book by the parent denomination.

The role of bulletins as tools of communication and education is something we have known about for years. Sometimes church bulletins are so cluttered with announcements and other information that even the side margins are filled. Bulletins provide a form for communication that is both up-to-date and short enough to maintain interest — maybe because most of the reading occurs during the sermon! Monthly parish newsletters, on the other hand, tend to be too lengthy, and most material is either dated too far in advance to be relevant or already out of date after the first week. Also, what appears in the newsletter frequently is a repetition of what appears in the bulletin anyway. Thus most parish newsletters, especially those stapled together, remain forever unopened. Recently some congregations have circumvented the mail box by providing weekly news updates via e-mail direct to congregational members.

We cannot underestimate how people save and reread bulletins. Many innovations in marriage services are the result of bulletins that couples have saved from various weddings they have attended. It is far more helpful for the couple planning a wedding to see what has been tried by others than simply for innovations to be suggested by the minister. The same can be said about bulletins for funerals and other occasional acts. Merely a stack of leftover bulletins in the narthex is enticement enough for people to pick them up and take them home to read. If somebody else has tried something new, there is less risk involved in trying it for oneself.

Prayer books and liturgies included in hymnals, even though they provide for alternatives, can change only every generation or so. Bulletins can change weekly. This does not mean that worship need be reduced to a collection of liturgical novelties. But it does mean that the liturgical expressions can reflect the needs of people at a given time and can be in harmony with the rhythm of the church year and special festivals. From a practical standpoint, it also means that each worshiper doesn't need thirty-seven fingers to flip from page to page and book to book in order to allow for variety and alternatives. Everything can be printed readily at hand without a lot of cluttering rubrics.

Hymnals, too, are usually out of date by the time they are released from the presses and suffer from a lack of inclusiveness caused by space limitations. The schedule for the introduction of a new hymnal is determined by the length of time it takes for the present ones to wear out and be rebound at least once. That's probably a time period of around twenty to thirty years, depending on how hard congregations are on their hymnals. Economics and the ability to hold a hymnal comfortably in one's hand dictate that only so many hymns are included — and that means many also are excluded. Bulletins are free from all these restrictions. Not all verses of all hymns need be or should be sung all the time. By printing in the bulletins only those verses to be sung, one avoids confusion. Even the melody line can be included. If a hymn is appropriate to the service and cannot be found in the hymnal, the words can easily be printed in the bulletins. Printing of the words allows for some hymns, depending upon an equal meter, to be sung to different tunes. Many hymns were not written to be sung to a specific tune in the first place, and carefully wedding one text to another tune can be quite exciting. There are several computerized music notation programs available that enable both the musical notes and the words of the texts to be created in a very professional-looking format. All this is possible via bulletins as long as one observes the copyrights. Again, there are a number of licensing agreements that provide, for a nominal yearly fee, the copyright clearances necessary for hymns still under copyright to be included in weekly bulletins.

A. B. Dick had no idea of the ramifications of his little machine. As a consequence of the mimeograph, liturgical expressions are by nature both more contemporaneous and more disposable than those distilled by the process involved in getting together new prayer books and hymnals. This does not mean that we need to be content with theologically shallow and liturgically shoddy expressions. But it does mean that, like a really good sermon, which can be preached only once, some expressions will need to be relegated to the ring binders after but one Sunday's use. And if the expressions are to be worthy for the worship of God, a lot of hard work will have to go into the preparation of each week's bulletin. The minister, as the crafter of corporate worship, is going to have to spend a larger portion of time creating a new prayer book each week, probably more time than may be spent on the sermon. And just as not every sermon is of publishable quality, perhaps a particular week's liturgical expressions are not going to be worth writing home about; but maybe next week's will be. That's why bulletins are both a blessing and a curse upon the minister. Yet electronic storage allows easy retrieval of those pieces worth using again when the three-year cycle of the lectionary engages those same biblical texts again.

I believe ultimately that bulletins are important because they are not only the medium for the message of each Sunday but also part of the message itself. We can thank the late Marshall McLuhan and others in the secular community for reminding us in secular terms of the liturgical reality that how we pray determines what we believe. Luther's *Deutsche Messe,* as a liturgical expression, was the medium for worship reformation, but it surely was the message of that reformation as well. Bulletins are part of the total worship experience. Hence they need to be designed purposely with the message in mind. They need to take into consideration the unintended messages as well. If people cannot read the print, this message will be negative. If the pages are jammed full of words, the message won't be able to get through the jungle. However, if Sunday bulletins are so arranged to be in harmony with the whole service, what is corporately enacted will have behind it a tremendously powerful tool. This never hit me until one day a member of a worship committee who was to articulate what was happening in some alternative services produced a cork-board full of bulletins from those services. I knew then very clearly that the medium is indeed the message.

Let's get on with some of the practicalities of the bulletin format. Too often what will be included in bulletins is dictated by the size of the covers made available to churches by ecclesiastical supply houses. These covers generally come in two varieties, neither of which is liturgically helpful. The first variety features a full-page photograph or drawing of either the interior or exterior of the church building. I see no practical purpose for this type of cover except to serve as a souvenir for tourists. The congregation knows what the building looks like, inside and out, and a front page reminder each week is a waste of precious space. The second variety of cover is produced by or for denominations, generally to foster denominational programs through what is printed on the back. Thus the usable space is restricted to the inside — one 8½ by 11–inch piece of paper folded in half. After space is allocated for parish announcements, the names of the participants in the service, the church staff, the donors of the flowers, and all the other *et cetera,* what remains for the liturgy is generally one half of the inside sheet. All that can appear in such a small space is a listing of the parts of the service with references to pages in the hymnal or prayer book where the various liturgical acts may be found. Liturgical renewal needs more space.

On the other hand, an 8½ by 14–inch sheet of paper folded in half, especially without a full-page picture on the front, provides the space necessary for the bulletin to become a weekly prayer book. The order of worship can begin on the front and continue on the inside. Additional pages can be folded and inserted inside in booklet style with a single staple in the spine to hold the booklet together. Even the denomination-ally produced covers can become the front and back of such a worship booklet.

The way in which the liturgical acts are included in the bulletin will mean the difference between a shopping list directory and a truly usable liturgy. The beginning section of many bulletins looks like this:

```
ORDER OF WORSHIP
 ORGAN PRELUDE
 CALL TO WORSHIP, No. 4, p. 130
*HYMN NO. 123
*CALL TO CONFESSION
*CONFESSION OF SIN, No. 1, p. 171
*WORDS OF ASSURANCE
*RESPONSIVE PSALM, No. 2, p. 253
```

I am sure that, except for the numbers, next week's bulletin will look exactly like this one — quite uninteresting. Moreover, the congregation will become distracted by the mechanics of flipping from page to page in the hymnal. Permit me to make some changes in the way the same material will appear. Unless there is some compelling reason why the organist's music needs to be identified, the name of the piece as well as the label "Organ Prelude" can be omitted. If the call to worship really expresses what it is meant to be, there is no need for this part of the gathering act to be identified; hence the label "Call to Worship" can be eliminated and the call can be printed directly. The worship leader will probably call the congregation to confession, so that label can be omitted also. The words of the confession can be printed directly in the bulletin, thereby eliminating the need for people to turn to another place in the hymnal or prayer book. Words of assurance will be spoken by the worship leader; thus that heading can be omitted also. The words of the Psalm, unless the Psalm is too lengthy, can be printed in the bulletin; the same can be said regarding the hymn.

Therefore, after my editorializing, the same order looks like this:

ORDER OF WORSHIP

Leader: This is the day the Lord has made!

All: Let us rejoice and be glad in it!

The congregation may stand.

HYMN NO. 123

CONFESSION OF SIN: *in unison*

> **Have mercy upon us, O God,**
> **according to your loving kindness:**
> **According to the multitude of your tender mercies**
> **blot out our transgressions.**
> **Wash us thoroughly from our iniquities,**
> **and cleanse us from our sins.**
> **For we acknowledge our transgressions,**
> **and our sin is ever before us.**
> **Create in us clean hearts, O God,**
> **and renew a right spirit within us;**
> **through Jesus Christ our Lord. Amen.**

Leader: Listen to the comforting assurance of the grace of God
promised in the Gospel to all who repent and believe:
Whoever is in Christ is a new creation:
everything old has passed away;
Behold, everything has become new!
All this is from God, who reconciled us through Christ,
and has given us the ministry of reconciliation.

— 1 Corinthians 5:17–18, alt.

All: We believe the good news! Thanks be to God!

PSALM:

Leader: O Lord, our Sovereign, how majestic is your name in all the earth!

All: You have set your glory above the heavens....

Of course, this takes more space, but what we have here is a liturgy, not just a list of labels. All that is necessary for congregational participation is printed; what isn't necessary is left out. A brief rubric about standing removes any uncertainty of when to stand and makes it unnecessary for the worship leader to "scoop up" the congregation somewhere during the introduction. It also makes asterisks unnecessary. If the stanzas of the hymn are not printed for lack of space, include (as in the above example) at least the first two lines to indicate what sort of hymn it is — in the example, a hymn of joyous praise. Printing prayers and other expressions in phrase form rather than in paragraphs preserves the original integrity — in the example, the Hebrew poetic lines — and facilitates corporate reading. When the words of hymns are included, the phrases can be carried over from one line to the next, thus eliminating the disjunctures sometimes caused by musical notation. For example, the third and fourth lines of one stanza of a familiar hymn looks like this in most hymnals:

**Hast thou not seen How thy desires e'er have been
Granted in what he ordaineth?**

By printing the words in a way that preserves the follow-through of the sentence, the expression has meaning:

Hast thou not seen how thy desires e'er have been granted in what he ordaineth?

Word processors have centering capabilities that not only make setup easier, but also eliminate the natural tendency to shove each line against the left margin — a habit left over from the typewriter era! If bulletins are what most people conceive them to be in the first place, some simple changes in the way liturgical expressions are printed will enable them to function better as worthy instruments of common prayer.

However, since bulletins are on an equal par with prayer books in the minds of many, we need to be sensitive to the ways we make changes. Even though the format of many bulletins may be cluttered with listings of labels, a revolution in that format overnight is tantamount to an official revision of the Book of Common Prayer. Change by evolution rather than revolution may be more acceptable. Maybe, for the time being, some of the labels must remain. Gradually, as people find them really unnecessary, some can be eliminated. The beauty of bulletins as opposed to bound prayer books is that they allow for growth and renewal to come from within the community itself rather than from changes forced upon the church by the arrival of new denominational hymnals or prayer books placed in the pews.

Finally, if worship committees in local churches serve a greater function than authorizing the purchase of candles and the scheduling of ushers, they need to be part of the process of determining what the congregation's worship will be. These committees ought to be allowed to share in shaping the liturgical expressions. The results, then, will not be liturgical novelties but true expressions of the church seeking to worship God in an authentic and honest way. Their language and cadences may not be equal to those labored over for generations by liturgical scholars and denominational commissions. But what one will find collected in the ring binders of bulletins over the years will be a uniquely beautiful treasury of worship vessels created by the people of God in the ongoing process of shaping the church's common prayer.

Appendix

Accompaniments

Kyrie

F. Russell Mitman, 2004

Lord, have mer - cy on us.

Christ, have mer - cy on us.

Lord, have mer - cy on us.

Psalm 139 Response

F. Russell Mitman, 2004

Lord, you have searched me and known me.

Kyrie with Amen

F. Russell Mitman, 1987

Lord, have mer - cy on us, Christ, have mer - cy on us,

Lord, have mer - cy on us. A - men.

Doxology from Revelation

F. Russell Mitman, 2000

Bless-ing and glo - ry and wis-dom and thanks and hon - or and pow - er and might be to God for

ev - er and ev - er more, for ev - er and ev - er more. A - men.

Glory to the Father

F. Russell Mitman, 2004

Glo - ry to the Fa - ther, and to the Son, and to the Ho - ly Spir - it:

as it was in the be - gin - ning, is now, and will be for - ev - er. A - men.

Gospel Versicles

F. Russell Mitman, 2003

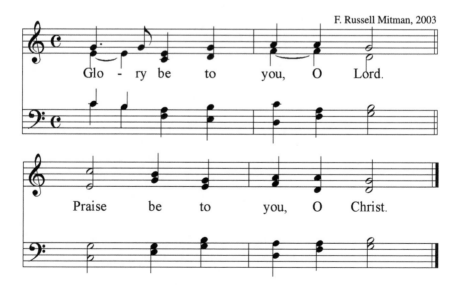

Glo - ry be to you, O Lord.

Praise be to you, O Christ.

Prayer Response

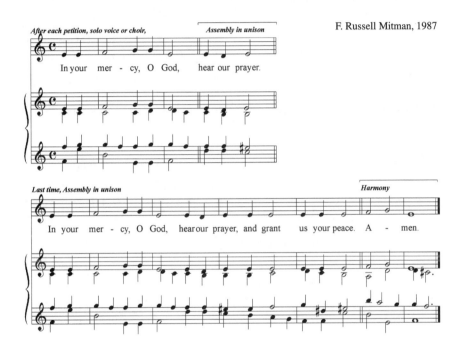

F. Russell Mitman, 1987

Accompaniment for
Stanzas 1 through 4

MAUNDY 8.8.8.8
F. Russell Mitmanm, 2004

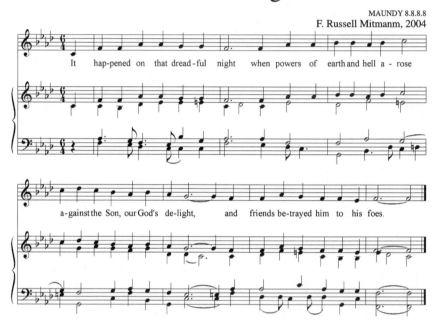

It hap-pened on that dread-ful night when powers of earth and hell a - rose

a-gainst the Son, our God's de-light, and friends be-trayed him to his foes.

Accompaniment for
Stanza 5 (Major Key)

MAUNDY 8.8.8.8

Isaac Watts, 1709, alt.

F. Russell Mitmanm, 2004

Jesus, Lamb of God

F. Russell Mitman, 2004

Doxology for
UCC Statement of Faith

F. Russell Mitman, 2004

Bless-ing   and   hon - or,   glo - ry   and

power   be   un - to   you!   A   -   men.

Sanctus and Benedictus
Accompaniment

F. Russell Mitman, 2001